ADVANCE PRAISE FOR *BUY THEN BUILD*

"A deftly written, exceedingly thorough, and highly informative business guide."

—KIRKUS REVIEWS

"Looking back twenty years from now, acquisition entrepreneurship will be as normal as going to law school today. In the meantime, it's a huge opportunity to hop on the train before the secret gets out, and Walker explains exactly how to do that."

—TAYLOR PEARSON, bestselling author of *The End of Jobs*

"In *Buy Then Build*, Walker Deibel creates a framework for entrepreneurs to capitalize on the biggest transfer of wealth in human history."

—VERNE HARNISH, Founder of Entrepreneurs' Organization (EO) and author of *Scaling Up (Rockefeller Habits 2.0)*

"We've grown our startup's value by over $30 million and added over a hundred accounts to cross-sell after implementing what we learned by reading *Buy Then Build*. If you're an entrepreneur and want to scale your business, this is a must-read."

—BRIAN HANDRIGAN, Co-Founder and CEO of Advocado

One of "7 Business Books Entrepreneurs Need to Read"

—FORBES

"I first met Walker shortly after his first acquisition. I then watched as he bought and sold over a half dozen companies while other entrepreneurs were building from scratch. Walker has uniquely expanded the toolbox for entrepreneurs, and *Buy Then Build* clearly outlines how to get started."

—JOHN RUHLIN, bestselling author and Co-Founder of GIFT•OLOGY

"*Buy Then Build* is a total game-changer. I wish all entrepreneurs would read this."

—JOE VALLEY, bestselling author of *The Exitpreneur's Playbook* and Managing Partner at Quiet Light

"Walker's book is a compelling (and accessible) introduction to the increasingly popular world of entrepreneurship through acquisition. A key addition to any aspiring ETA entrepreneur's reading list."

—DAVID SCHONTHAL, *Wall Street Journal* bestselling co-author of *The Human Element*, award-winning professor, and Director of Entrepreneurship Programs at the Kellogg School of Management

"*Buy Then Build* is a practical guide to cash flow investing, business, and improving financial IQ. I recommend this book to all of our clients."

—GARRETT GUNDERSON, *New York Times* bestselling author of *Killing Sacred Cows* and Founder of Wealth Factory

"Walker clearly shows how acquisitions and entrepreneurship are not mutually exclusive but coexist as value builders. *Buy Then Build* is required reading for anyone aspiring to build, or buy, their own business."

—KARY OBERBRUNNER, CEO of Igniting Souls and *Wall Street Journal* and *USA Today* bestselling author

"Walker is playing it smart. He sees opportunities others don't."

—CLIFF HOLEKAMP, former Director of Entrepreneurship at Washington University in St. Louis and Co-Founder of Cultivation Capital

"Walker Deibel is an acquisition genius. First, he acquired $16 million in business revenue across seven businesses—learning and then *mastering* all the tricks of the trade along the way. The best part is he clearly documents his system inside *Buy Then Build*. He has helped hundreds of other entrepreneurs acquire successful businesses with his easy-to-follow method. Reading *Buy Then Build* is insight into an entrepreneur who has lived where few have gone."

—**STEVE NIXON**, online entrepreneur and investor

"Walker is the real deal, and he shares his insights for running a successful company from day one."

—**SHEP HYKEN**, *New York Times* bestselling author of *The Amazement Revolution*

"Some people have suggested I write a book on buying a small business, which is why I was excited to see Walker Deibel had just saved me the trouble!"

—**JOHN WARRILLOW (VIA TWITTER)**, bestselling author of *Built to Sell, The Automatic Customer,* and *The Art of Selling Your Business* and creator of The Value Builder System

"*Buy Then Build* clearly outlines the framework for capturing value through acquisitions."

—**MARK DAOUST**, Founder of Quiet Light Brokerage

"*Buy Then Build* should have been taught in every MBA program."

—**CODIE SANCHEZ**, Founder of Contrarian Thinking, private equity investor, and owner of twenty-six businesses

"Walker spent over a decade perfecting his approach to small business acquisition *before* authoring his bestseller on the subject. *Buy Then Build* has reframed business acquisitions for a new generation of entrepreneurs. It's a pioneering work in the exploding practice of entrepreneurship through acquisition."

—DOUG VILLARD, Academic Director for Entrepreneurship at the Olin School of Business and Managing Partner at Villard Growth Partners

"*Buy Then Build* has already been called superb, enlightening, and inspirational. I can't say anything better!"

—TOM WEST, Co-Founder of Business Brokerage Press and IBBA

BUY
THEN
BUILD

How Acquisition Entrepreneurs
Outsmart the Startup Game

WALKER DEIBEL

COPYRIGHT © 2018 WALKER DEIBEL

All rights reserved.

BUY THEN BUILD

How Acquisition Entrepreneurs

Outsmart the Startup Game

ISBN   978-1-5445-3566-1   Hardcover

       978-1-5445-0113-0   Paperback

       978-1-5445-0114-7   Ebook

LIONCREST
PUBLISHING

IN MEMORY OF BOB DEIBEL
your grandfather's entrepreneur

MASTER ACQUISITION ENTREPRENEURSHIP

Go to BUYTHENBUILD.COM to get bonus materials, access
additional resources, watch expert interviews, join the
private community, and more.

CONTENTS

FOREWORD

BY CHAD TROUTWINE

ONE BRISK SPRING MORNING IN 2011, I ARRIVED AT MY MALIBU beachfront office to find a film crew waiting to interview me. They explained that they were there to film a promotional video for Corley Printing, Walker Deibel's very first buy-then-build success story. I had no memory of agreeing to do any such thing (and still don't), but that occasionally happens to me. Whenever I agree to do something far into the future, I just say yes and imagine the day will never come. But this time, the day had come and it was today. As a person worthy of being the star of a micro-budget promotional video, I had a hundred more important things to do that morning. I would have weaseled out of the shoot (or at least changed into a more stylish outfit), but I truly loved Corley Printing and their dynamic young CEO, so with a broad a smile, I said, "Mic me up, fellas!"

Just as most everyone under fifty years old was running from anything having to do with the printing industry, Walker had gone against the grain and actually acquired a book manufacturing company. I got a front row seat to watch as he made decisions that transformed the company, and quickly became a regional leader in digital book production—perhaps the only area that was growing under the changing printing landscape. Under Walker's leadership, the company withstood the storm that hit the industry, became one of the largest 2 percent of printing companies in the United States, and experienced an exit.

Walker is more than just an author, and *Buy Then Build* is more than just some academic exercise. This book is an insider's look into a proven system, masterfully told by a veteran entrepreneur. Walker has already found success several times buying and building businesses. Just as the practice of entrepreneurship through acquisition is taking hold in business schools, Walker—if you'll forgive the obvious pun—is not just talking the talk; he has already walked the walk.

HIDDEN IN PLAIN SIGHT

Before I moved to California, I spent my childhood in suburban Kansas City, Missouri. No one I knew ever used the phrase "entrepreneur" to describe their job. Instead, folks used the much more modest description, "small business owner." Even as a child, I could tell theirs was the path for me (and not just because they tended to live in the biggest homes in the neighborhood). The businesses weren't glamorous—metal fabricating shops, car dealerships, local newspapers—but they looked fun, and I could see the value they provided to our town. As I grew older, I learned to appreciate the distinction between launching a startup and running a small business. They both have their appeal, but lately people seem to be over-hyping the former and deeply underappreciating the latter.

A CONTRARIAN PERSPECTIVE

Billionaire investor Peter Thiel is fond of asking people, "What important truth do very few people agree with you on?" Walker shares a fantastic answer in *Buy Then Build*: ambitious entrepreneurs should buy an existing company and use it as a platform to build value, rather than start a business from scratch. There are three primary reasons:

1. Startups have a little flaw: they mostly fail.

2. Existing companies have the established infrastructure that many startups are trying to build in the first place.

3. Acquisition entrepreneurs should match their resources and talent to transitioning businesses to create significant value in a company all their own.

Fortunately for you, Walker was not content with simply offering up generic advice. Instead he provides detailed, step-by-step instructions on how to buy then build your business. He compellingly makes the case that existing businesses offer an inherent advantage because they provide a profit-generating infrastructure, a pool of existing customers, an operational history, and experienced employees. Walker explains how to define your search and excel based on opportunity and discretionary earnings, rather than simply following the herd with business search tools that leave many would-be buyers never reaching success. He shares advice on how to navigate a deal, offers insight into what to expect from the seller, and even provides guidance on what your transition to CEO might look like.

Walker is one of the most important influences on my professional life. Through the pages of this superb book, he will enlighten, delight, and inspire you. *Buy Then Build* is a blueprint to constructing your own masterpiece. And you might even end up starring in a promotional video for it one day.

PART 1

OPPORTUNITY

"No army can withstand the strength of
an idea whose time has come."

—Victor Hugo

CHAPTER 1

DON'T START A BUSINESS

"IT'S DEAD."

John was the former director of product management for Microsoft Services and now acted as the CEO of our startup, ViewPoint. He was referring to our company. "We're out of cash, the product isn't functional, and we don't have any paying customers. It's over."

This wasn't my first startup. Or even my first startup failure. I understood the risks—indeed, after having a previous startup fail, I thought I had learned the variables that lead to a successful launch. This time was going to be different.

We not only had a great product in a fast-growing market, but an all-star team. Our largest investor was a former Fortune 500 CEO. Our own CEO had been the SharePoint consulting executive at Microsoft and had worked with customers directly in our target market. Our team of proven, high-revenue-generating developers had built successful enterprise software before, and one of our advisors was a CTO of a Fortune 500 company. The equity raise was oversubscribed, and within months of graduating from one of the top-ten startup accelerator programs in the world we had beta trials inside many recognizable companies. We had all the hallmarks of success...but no actual success.

Startups have an inherent flaw: they mostly fail. Even with over-whelming talent, outstanding early product trials, and an all-star team, success is still unlikely. We've all heard the statistic that one out of ten startups make it. It's not a secret. We all go in with two eyes open. It appeared that ViewPoint was no exception.

The goal for entrepreneurs is to run and operate a successful business. The goal for investors is to make money by investing in a successful business. There's just one problem—the startup phase is a company killer.

Data suggests that, at best, only half of all startups make it past this stage. Those that do often come out not looking like Uber, but more like a small business. As Verne Harnish, author of *Scaling Up*, observes, only 4 percent of all companies in the United States ever exceed $1 million in revenue.[1] It's odd to me that despite the interest in entrepreneurship, we really haven't engineered a better way to avoid the startup runway and build sustainability into startups from the beginning. When we drill down into the numbers on this level, we're left with the stark fact that somewhere well north of 99 percent of all startups either fail completely, or never really amount to much—either financially or impactfully.

What if there was a way to establish success from the beginning? An "entrepreneurship hack," so to speak. A path that could bypass the startup phase altogether, so entrepreneurs could start operating a successful business as the Chief Executive Officer from day one. This would provide an immediate platform to add value from. You)uld grow it, run it as is, or use the cash flow from the company fund the creation of new products or services.

This exists, and it's called *acquisition entrepreneurship*.

---

rnish, Verne (2014), *Scaling Up: How a Few Companies Make It...and Why the Don't*. Ashburn, VA: Gazelles Inc.

ACQUISITION ENTREPRENEURSHIP

Acquisition entrepreneurs start by buying an existing business instead of starting one from scratch. From there, they bring an entrepreneurial approach to build value. The combination of an existing small business' profitable and sustainable infrastructure with the innovation and drive of an entrepreneur is a magical recipe.

The main benefit of acquisition entrepreneurship is that existing companies are already established with customers, brand awareness, employees, and most importantly, revenue and profits—everything a startup doesn't have.

Instead of having to raise money for months (often *years*) while also trying to build sales from scratch with a new product, the acquisition entrepreneur acquires a profitable infrastructure from which to begin. Existing businesses provide established markets, so they don't have to worry whether they are too early or whether another company with more funding will beat them to market share—or in some cases, worry about *creating* a market from scratch. Simply by buying a company, typically one greater than $1 million in revenue, you can remove so much of the risk inherent to entrepreneurship.

Further, many successful small businesses have been operating for decades. This means their model for success was developed a long time ago, and many of these businesses could benefit from the fresh approach and skillset of the next generation of entrepreneurs. There is a lot of opportunity inside small companies that operate on legacy systems, never upgraded to lean business models, or never developed sales teams or effective online marketing.

Following ViewPoint's capitulation,[2] an advisor who helped me exit my previous company found a print management and

---

2   We did actually sell the ViewPoint product and codebase to a proven firm that I expect will do extremely well with it.

distribution company that he thought would be a good fit. The company was selling a few million in revenue and had a handful of noteworthy, highly-respected, and well-known clients.

Through our analysis—although print management and centralized "brand control" was valuable to its customers—we decided that the real core competency of the business was in its inventory management and fulfillment capabilities, which provides its customers the benefits of lean supply chain management practices. It was clear that the product lines could be easily expanded.

Indeed, one of the biggest clients came to the seller and asked if he could put other products important to their supply chain into the online ordering system. We saw the potential to build a true business-to-business fulfillment company from the existing infrastructure, providing a private and customized "Amazon-like experience" for companies with multiple locations.

I acquired the company in early 2015 with a low six-figure investment and a bank loan. After the closing, and with the cash flow from the company, we hired part-time software engineers and created a proprietary eCommerce storefront, which we quickly rolled out to tens of thousands of users nationwide—*everything we had tried but failed to achieve at ViewPoint.*

They were thrilled. Instead of an "online system," they now had a user-friendly website that didn't require training. Headquarters provided real time tracking metrics and accounting codes for their internal accounting system. We also implemented procedures that proactively managed inventory, which increased on time delivery of goods and confidence with the existing customer base.

In the first eleven months, my team more than doubled the marketable value of the company, simply by bringing a complimentary level of innovation into an established and stable business.

To fuel the fire even further, I acquired a local promotional and corporate apparel business the following year. We merged it into the fulfillment company, giving it an immediate 20 percent revenue boost and an additional 500 customers. This too was funded by the cash flow of the business I had already acquired.

The venture was a clear example of the power of acquisition entrepreneurship. While we failed to get enough paying users at ViewPoint—despite lots of capital, a beloved and innovative product, and a ridiculously accomplished team—I was able to achieve the same end goal by acquiring a successful business and then using the cash flow to innovate and upgrade the offering and the talent. This was accomplished at a fraction of the cost and a fraction of the time, and provided 100 percent ownership of the company.

Moreover, this was not the first time I had done business this way. Over the past ten years since then, I've acquired seven different companies and made minority investments in more. These have included book printing, distribution, promotional product companies, eCommerce, education, and metal fabrication and finishing. All of them had growth opportunities for those who could identify them and who understood acquisition entrepreneurship. I bought these businesses because I believed I, or my team, could add value to them.

I've been lucky. I've navigated it fairly well and, most of the time, made them more valuable than when I bought them. I've even been fortunate enough to experience a successful exit through this process—the crown jewel achievement of all startups.

Practicing acquisition entrepreneurship flips the startup model on its head. Instead of building the infrastructure and then working to find the revenue to support it, it seeks profitable revenue first. By doing so, the startup runway is eliminated, allowing for immediate focus on activities that improve an already successful enterprise. Activities like managing, innovating, and growing the company start on day one.

Compare this to raising capital by selling company stock while simultaneously trying to find product/market fit...all while under the stress of managing a cash flow negative burn. It's no wonder startup founders sometimes confuse equity investment with revenue.

There are roughly 500,000[3] small businesses acquired each year. These acquisition entrepreneurs are skipping the startup phase altogether, unlocking trillions in value, and living the successful entrepreneur lifestyle.

ACQUISITION IS MORE AFFORDABLE THAN YOU THINK

I can hear you already. "I could never do this because I'm not rich."

First, I'd say that in my experience, very few entrepreneurs raising capital to launch startups are rich, so I'm not sure the comparison is all that valid. That said, and although brokers typically want to see a few hundred thousand in available cash, it's the nature of buying an existing business that makes it much easier to gain access to capital.

Banks offer loans to buyers for up to 90 percent of the purchase price, using the assets of the business as collateral. Remember I mentioned raising capital takes a fraction of the time? The financing of these deals is typically done in one fell swoop, with you bringing a "down payment" or "equity infusion" and the bank providing the balance.

In addition, raising money from a bank also means that you get to own 100 percent of the company yourself.

---

3   *https://www.bizbuysell.com/news/article084.html*

If you require investors or other backing for the initial equity infusion, you have options. You can bring on partners, raise from friends and family, or pitch family offices or angel investors who will be attracted to the better economics when compared to start-ups. There has also been an increasing trend in new search funds. These funds are dedicated to helping acquisition entrepreneurs buy businesses. These funds can also assist in helping you acquire significantly larger companies than you could do on your own, effectively allowing you to stretch well into the middle market (which I'll define here, as those companies generating between $5 and $100 million in revenue[4]) or provide additional capital to lower the debt profile.

All in all, buying a business is way more affordable than you think. In terms of initial capital required by the entrepreneur, it looks amazingly comparable to either starting a company or buying a house. Let me explain.

Babson College statisticians reported through the *Wall Street Journal* that the average startup in the US kicks off with $65,000 in invested capital. Similarly, the average down payment on a home for the last three years[5] was approximately $57,000, with the twenty-five counties experiencing the biggest increase in millennials[6] averaging $66,174. So, whether people are starting a business from scratch or buying a house, they are investing somewhere around $65,000.

Because companies under about $10 million in revenue tend to sell for lower multiples than middle-market or publicly traded

---

4   And yes, $100 million in revenue is still considered a small business by the US Bureau of Labor and Statistics.

5   Blomquist, Daren, June 2015, *www.Realtytrac.com.*

6   *https://www.housingwire.com/articles/33255-realtytrac-what-was-the-average-downpayment-in-2014*

companies, a $65,000 investment, paired with a 90 percent loan backed by the small business administration, could buy a company generating over $1 million in revenue, immediately launching an acquisition entrepreneur into the role of CEO of one of the largest 4 percent of companies in the US.

In loose math it would look like this (and to simplify, let's assume this equation does not include working capital, inventory, closing costs, or real estate):

$65,000 invested plus 90 percent SBA loan equals a $650,000 purchase price.

A company of that size is commonly acquired around a multiple of three times adjusted earnings.[7]

Adjusted earnings therefore are $216,000 ($650,000 divided by three).

Assuming a 15 percent adjusted earnings-to-revenue ratio, this company is generating over $1.4 million in revenue.

There are a lot of assumptions in a back-of-the-napkin calculation, but here the goal is to illustrate that an investment similar in size to starting a business from scratch or buying a house can instead be used to acquire a sustaining business generating profitable revenue with an existing infrastructure. There will be additional

---

7   "Adjusted earnings" here represents Adjusted EBITDA or Seller Discretionary Earnings, which will be explained later in the book. In short, it represents total Owner Benefit to be used for principal and interest payments, reinvestment, or salaries.

costs, but the takeaway is that it is absolutely achievable to acquire a company of this size with less than $100,000.

Rethinking how we approach entrepreneurship requires some tweaking of skillsets. Not as much in eliminating and adding, but rather the order in which they are mastered. Like all business professionals, acquisition entrepreneurs need to be a hybrid of investor and entrepreneur mentalities. As a first-time entrepreneur builds out their business plan, they quickly realize the need to be able to understand how to think like an investor in order to create a sustainable business and provide returns for the capital used to build the infrastructure to begin with.

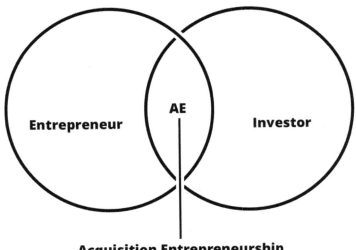

Acquisition Entrepreneurship

What's different about an acquisition model is that the entrepreneur needs to think and act as an investor before getting started. This engineers stronger, more sustainable companies and better entrepreneurs. In the illustration above, we outlined a $65,000 initial investment, generating over $200,000 in discretionary earnings to a buyer. It will be the investor mindset that will need to evaluate whether this is a good financial decision,[8] and to analyze the business' opportunity. As an entrepreneur, you'll be looking for an opportunity that is a fit for you, as well as something that has personal interest.

This means that the acquisition entrepreneur will need to learn how to manage and operate an existing company, simultaneous to being able to focus on innovation alone. These are skills that all successful entrepreneurs need to master as they move from creator to CEO, but the order in which they are addressed here is reversed—starting instead as CEO on an existing business, then bringing innovation, updates, and growth from there.

By combining an investment in the existing revenue, infrastructure, and earnings with the drive and innovation fueling the entrepreneur, acquisition provides a powerful recipe, allowing existing companies to go to new heights, having tremendous impact, and providing a platform for the entrepreneur's art.

ACQUISITION ENTREPRENEURSHIP VERSES VENTURE CAPITAL

Acquisition entrepreneurship is not right for every circumstance or everyone. After all, certain entrepreneurs have enjoyed such remarkable success that they have obtained celebrity, even legendary status. We're all familiar with the titans of technology who dominate the business media: Bill Gates, Steve Jobs, Jeff Bezos, Mark Zuckerberg, and Elon Musk, to name a few. These guys didn't start by buying a company, so why should you?[9]

---

8   Hint: if maintained, then this is a phenomenal return and unparalleled to any other investment vehicle. (More on this in Chapter 2.)

9   Actually, Musk did acquire PayPal when his own payment processing company failed. He also did not technically start Tesla either. Rather, he financed the growth

Lately, it's been the startups able to get to the billion-dollar valuation, the "unicorn" companies, in the limelight. These companies are changing how we live and work, and they are not only creating tremendous value but are introducing new business models. Indeed, all startups today aim to be the "Uber of [enter your industry here]," right?

All these companies sourced venture capital (VC) to launch their companies. If we have engineered a better way to start from scratch, it probably looks a lot like this. The average successful VC-backed startup raises $41 million. That's a lot of money and must solve a lot of problems.

According to Harvard Business School lecturer, Shikhar Ghosh, even VC-funded startups—the ones that every MBA startup strives to attain—have a 75 percent *failure* rate. So, extremely well-financed startups with the support of the best investment teams in the world are successful in doubling the already minuscule success rate of non-VC-backed startups. But the large majority of these companies still never make it to sustainability.

The VC game is one of portfolio management. Meaning there needs to be a sizeable enough portfolio for VC backing to make sense. This is why, as of 2008, the average VC fund is $350 million.[10] This provides capital for eight to fourteen companies per fund. Three winners pay for the fund and its return, while nine entrepreneurs get a shot "at bat" in a game that only accepts home runs. As an investor, you might like this game. Lots lose, but the few that win provide exceptional returns for you.

---

and took over as CEO. It wasn't until later that he was considered a cofounder of the company, for which he was sued by the original founder. Further, every other CEO on that list has acquired companies, most commonly to expand. Facebook did nothing with VR, for example, until it acquired Oculus.

10   Basil Peters, "Venture Capital Firms Are Too Big," *AngelBlog* 2013 post, graphs 1–3.

As an entrepreneur, you need to understand that you are not invested in the portfolio. You are invested in a specific company, so the economic advantages gained by the VC are not extended to you, and there is a very quantifiable 75 percent chance that your specific company will be a loser. It turns out, for the entrepreneur, VC isn't all it's cracked up to be.

I share this not to crush the dreams of entrepreneurs everywhere but to share insight into what engineering success might actually look like. Understanding that unicorn companies are more anecdotal than typical is simply a prerequisite. Starting a VC-backed company believing that you will be the next magazine cover success story is possible. But it might just be punishment for not understanding statistics.

Many believe that these high profile, fast growing companies are the ones driving the economy and new jobs. They do drive *trends* by placing significant bets on adolescent markets, but it's not actually where growth comes from.

WHERE GROWTH REALLY COMES FROM

In 1979, economist David Birch revealed that small businesses are responsible for creating the large majority of new jobs in his statistical report, *The Job Generation Process*. After release of the report, Birch continued to refine his findings, eventually settling on the term "gazelles" to define the 2–3 percent of companies that create 70 percent of new jobs every year.

Gazelles are defined by rapid growth and not size. To be classified as a gazelle, a company must have a starting revenue of at least $1 million, then grow at a rate of 20 percent every year for four years, resulting in the company doubling in size during that time.

Gazelles as job creation vehicles beat out the elephants (Fortune 500, think Wal-Mart or ExxonMobil) and mice (Main Street), which perhaps is a bit of a non-applicable comparison since the latter is defined by size instead of growth rate, so either could exist as a gazelle. That said, most gazelles are found neither on Wall Street nor Main Street, but in the middle market.

When forced to think of a gazelle, you might be tempted to think of technology companies. After all, isn't tech synonymous with high growth? Well, in the 1990s, yes. Zoltan Acs, director of the Center for Entrepreneurship and Public Policy at George Mason University, released his findings in 2008 that supported the notion that there were more gazelles in the tech industry in the 1990s than any other industry. However, in the 2000s, the leading industry was housing-related services.[11] I can speak to this myself, since our aluminum railing company grew at over 38 percent in 2017. Hardly high tech.

Acs observed that gazelles are found in all industries. Birch supports these observations highlighting that about a third of gazelles are found in wholesale and retail, and a third in the services industry. *Inc. Magazine* recognized this trend as well, publishing an article that compared their celebrated *Inc.* 500 companies to gazelles, recognizing that only 47 percent were tech related back in 2000.[12]

Sizable, to be sure, but the *Inc.* 5000 list only requires a $100,000 in revenue starting point—a tenth of the size of gazelles. Further, only 7.3 percent of the *Inc.* 5000 in 2016 were in the computer hardware or software industries. This is indicative that tech-related companies might have an edge in the "not failing" category, but find

---

11   http://www.forbes.com/forbes/2009/1116/careers-small-businesses-unemployment-hunting-for-gazelles.html

12   http://www.inc.com/magazine/20010515/22613.html

their place in the masses quickly thereafter. More likely, technology plays an important role in a company's productivity, but delivering high-tech products and services doesn't make it any more likely that a company will continue to be healthy in and of itself. After all, Acs' findings report that a mere 2–3 percent of all companies ever reach gazelle status, and none of them stay there forever.

One of Acs' findings could be surprising to fans of the "fast growth is only found in startups" myth. During a 2009 interview with Forbes, Acs revealed that *gazelles tend to be twenty-five years old*. These are the economy's most productive enterprises—and they're clearly not new companies coming out of accelerator programs. Instead, these are established, long-time companies.

Further, and contrary to popular belief, one researcher found there was a better way to dominate new industries, rather than fighting an incumbent with a new, disruptive offering.

THE PATH TO DOMINATING NEW INDUSTRIES

An existing company with legacy systems and an outdated path to success has just as much need for innovation as a startup does. As a result, those who can recognize and execute this can capitalize on the benefit of an existing platform to build in the "new company" they wish to run.

Consultant and bestselling author Jim Collins examines what causes companies to succeed or fail. His book, *How the Mighty Fall*, is a guide to understanding a company's various stages of decline and becoming better equipped to reverse the tide.

As we've seen in established companies like Blockbuster and Borders, all established organizations are vulnerable to missing an innovative trend. Collins explains how existing businesses that are able to embrace the disruptive technologies attacking them actually have a *better* rate of dominating the newcomers.

In fact, it's the old dogs with new tricks that have a higher probability of withstanding disruption within their markets. The old dogs have the benefit of existing revenue and earnings. They have infrastructure and invaluable industry insight. They have customers wanting to update to the trends.

It's testament that the challenges startups face never really go away, and that having infrastructure generating profitable revenue is the best possible tool for innovating. It's the combination of innovation and existing customers that wins in the war of disruptive technologies.

Realizing that venture capital might not be the best resource for engineering a successful company, and pairing that with an understanding that the strongest growth is actually more commonly found in established industries, lends itself to some of the advantages of starting with acquisition. What does all this mean for today's would-be entrepreneurs?

Luckily, there happens to be a once-in-history opportunity occurring right now.

THE $10 TRILLION TSUNAMI

The baby boomer generation owns more businesses than any other generation ever in history.

In 2013, they owned 12 million small businesses, which is 43 percent of all small businesses in the country.[13] That same year, they also started to retire at a rate of 9,000 per day.

The rate in which boomers are retiring is going to increase significantly over the next eighteen years. By 2021, baby boomers

---

13   *https://www.worldwealthreport.com/*

will be retiring at a rate of 11,000 per day. Almost 77 million people, about 20 percent of the US population, are going to retire between 2013 and 2029, and it is estimated that $10 trillion in existing business value[14] will need to change hands.

The boomers are already selling off their established, successful small businesses at record rates.[15] These businesses provide an unprecedented opportunity for acquisition entrepreneurs to focus on running, growing, and innovating a business *immediately*, all while enjoying a stability not found in startups.

This substantial increase in supply of available businesses for sale is expected to result in a buyer's market like we've never seen. This means the infrastructure built by generations before will be available for purchase at the most affordable levels ever experienced.

Most people simply don't understand that you can buy a substantial and scalable existing business for under $100,000 down. Couple that with the retiring baby boomer population and we've got a ripe environment for acquisition entrepreneurship to thrive like never before.

GETTING STARTED

So where do you start? How do you learn how to successfully buy a business?

The idea for this book came to me in 2004 after graduating from a top MBA program. A few of us launched a startup in graduate school, and despite the fact that we performed extremely well in

---

14   Richard Jackim and Peter Chritman, *The $10 Trillion Opportunity: Designing Successful Exit Strategies for Middle Market Business Owners*, Palatine, IL, The Exit Planning Institute.

15   *http://mobile.nytimes.com/2015/08/20/business/smallbusiness/baby-boomers-ready-to-sell-businesses-to-the-next-generation.html?referer=&_r=0*

business plan competitions, the company floundered in legal hang-ups during our last semester.

I knew I wanted to own and operate my own company, but I didn't have a compelling idea for a startup, so I started looking for a small business to acquire. I had no money and no idea where to start. There weren't any high-quality resources on the subject, and my world-class MBA education hadn't offered insight into this area.

I tried meeting with business brokers to see what I could learn. Most of them rightly assumed I had very little capital to invest and tried to sell me a downward-trending bar or a laundromat. I discovered a fragmented industry with few rules, zero best practices, little reliable information, and a huge variance in the quality of available opportunities.

Further, business brokers and M&A Advisors[16] are not terribly incentivized to hold the hands of first-time buyers. It's wrong of me to categorize all of them, but unsurprisingly, they are commonly looking for the biggest deals with the biggest fish. They've also been run through the ringer by working with buyers who can't close. So, at minimum they want the confidence to know that they have a buyer who can execute without bank financing, since they won't get paid for months and don't want the added risk of a buyer who can't execute. Like all industries, there are great brokers out there, but it took me years to know where to find them or how to evaluate them.

I needed a high-quality source of information for how to acquire an existing company, but it didn't exist. Acquisition

---

16 The terms Business Brokers, Intermediaries, M&A Advisors, and Investment Bankers are all titles for professionals who execute almost identical services. Although Business Brokers tends to have a "Main Street" connotation and I-Banker a "Wall Street," if you want to buy a company with a couple million in revenue, you will find people with all four of these titles. As a result, I use them interchangeably throughout the book.

entrepreneurship is not taught in most schools. Unless you're one of the fortunate few, lucky enough to participate in one of the very recently developed, top-tier programs at Harvard, Northwestern, University of Chicago, or Stanford, the resources for learning this approach are limited. Instead, I spent the last decade molding a process based on my experiences and now want to share them.

I won't pretend that acquiring a company is not a big deal. It's a significant event. It's hard, it can be complicated, and like anything involving money, it's emotional and risky. In fact, almost everybody who starts down the path of acquiring a business never pulls the trigger. I believe the reason is that they lack a process to get them from where they are today to where they want to go. There is no compass for building a search plan, sourcing deals, evaluating intermediaries, learning what to look out for, or finding the real opportunity in an offer. Often, there are no intimately known examples of others who have done it before you. What if your analysis is flawed or there is a pitfall you're not seeing?

I hope this book (and *BuyThenBuild.com*) can help solve this problem. It's meant to be the resource that I needed when I started, so I could skip the startup phase, gain confidence, and move right into ownership of a profitable company.

This book isn't limited to my experience alone. I've interviewed and incorporated experiences and research from world-class institutions, investors, private equity managers, and all types of entrepreneurs. The result is a framework unlike anything I've seen anywhere else.

With luck, we can evolve how people think about entrepreneurship and unlock the huge opportunity for more people to be entrepreneurs by leveraging the tremendous value in the existing small business economy.

One more thing: the information is all here, but just reading a book won't do it. You need to commit your time to taking action. You need to commit to investing your own money and betting on yourself. You need to be willing to create a business plan and pitch it to banks or other potential investors. Finally, you need to be comfortable and willing to take calculated risks. Although we're paving the way to a greater success rate for entrepreneurs, you are still the most important part of the equation.

Buy Then Build will explore the opportunity available right now in detail and give you a blueprint for building your search process, evaluating deals, and executing the acquisition phase. This is the roadmap for anyone with the drive to take the acquisition entrepreneur path, to become CEO of their own company through buying, then building their business.

First, understand small business as an investment vehicle.

CHAPTER 2

ENGINEERING WEALTH

ACCORDING TO THOMAS STANLEY AND WILLIAM DANKO, authors of the best-selling book, *The Millionaire Next Door*, effectively 100 percent of non-retired millionaires who live in the United States own their own businesses. Out of that group, about 20 percent are professionals running a medical or service business, and the balance are entrepreneurs and small business owners.

John Bowen, CEO of CEG Worldwide and coauthor of *The State of the Affluent*,[17] concluded through his research that some 80 percent of the affluent are either retired or own their own company. Further, an astounding 91 percent of everyone having over $5 million in net worth owns their own company—a trend suggesting that the wealthier someone is, the more likely they are to own a business.

Owning your own business is not only an opportunity to provide value through products and services, but it's arguably the best way for most people to build real wealth. In this chapter, we'll look at acquisition entrepreneurship as an investment vehicle.

---

17   *http://www.cegworldwide.com/downloads/ebwp/eread/SOA/State_of_the_Affluent.pdf.*
Bowen concluded that 50 percent of the affluent are retired and 30 percent could be categorized as either entrepreneurs or business owners.

To be clear, this does not mean that after you buy a business you are promised a high net-worth ranking. Nor does it mean that acquiring a company *purely* for financial gain is a good idea. Rather, it points to the fact that being the owner of a successful business can be a great investment vehicle, and that those who make the most of it can finish big.

We've seen that the acquisition entrepreneur needs to act as both entrepreneur and investor. After all, by utilizing the bank instead of private investors for the majority of financing, it puts the responsibility on the entrepreneur to invest their own money into the company. At a minimum, you'll want to understand the basic rules of investing before you start looking at potential acquisitions.

WHAT MAKES A GOOD INVESTMENT?

Luckily for us, entire industries have been built around investing in alternative assets such as startups and existing businesses— namely, venture capital and private equity. The investment strategies found in real estate investing also hold a fundamentally analogous approach to business buying. That of using leverage along with an initial equity investment to acquire an asset.

But what makes for a good investment?

While considering acquisitions as an investment, keep three fundamentals in mind: return on investment, margin of safety, and upside potential.

RETURN ON INVESTMENT

The concept of return on investment (ROI) is simple. If you invest $100 and it generates $6 back to you every year, then every year that you own that asset you will receive a 6 percent ROI.[18]

---

18   Six dollars received annually divided by the investment of $100 is 6 percent.

Let's say you sell that asset after seven years. Luckily, it's worth more than when you bought it, so you sell it for $120. During the seven years you owned it, you made $6 every year, or $42. Adding the $20 increase in value of the asset you realized when you sold it, you made a total of $62 on a $100 investment over seven years.[19] This equates to an 8.9 percent annual ROI during the life of the investment ($62/seven years).

Simple right?

Let's break down what just happened. During the seven years of ownership, the asset returned $6 back to you in cash. Let's call this "cash flow," or the amount of cash coming back to you as the owner of the asset.

When you bought the asset for $100 and sold it for $120 seven years later, the value of the asset itself increased during that time. In real estate, this is called *appreciation*. In the illustration above, the increase in value of the asset made up about a third of the total return.

When evaluating a potential acquisition, the cash flow the company generates is what sets the sale price of the company. It's the driver behind the valuation and ultimately what you're paying for. Anything outside of the company's ability to generate cash is commonly not worth paying for at all. At its core, what you are buying is an asset that provides cash flow.

The next logical question then is how much cash flow should a certain investment return? The answer is found in the risk profile of the investment. A United States-backed treasury bond is considered about as safe of an investment as possible. Today, they are generating 2.5–3 percent on invested capital, or enough to keep up with expected inflation during the time of ownership, but not much more.

---

19 Six dollars per year for seven years, plus the twenty dollars at exit equal sixty-two dollars.

Conversely, a startup is considered one of the riskiest investments around. And rightfully so. As we've seen, the infrastructure, proof of concept, product market fit, and revenue all need to be built from zero. That translates as any return to an investor is unlikely, so the average positive return needs to be very high to compensate for the risk.

A business with under $5 million in revenue and a track record of positive ongoing cash flow for fifteen years is somewhere in the middle. It's significantly safer than a startup, but not nearly as secure as a US-backed security.

The larger a company, the safer an investment is considered. This is because it's easier for a Main Street company to go out of business than a Fortune 500 company. As a result, companies under $1 million in revenue might sell for two to three times their cash flow, while large, publicly traded companies comfortably trade at a price-to-earnings ratio in the twenties or well beyond. You can buy McDonald's or Apple today on the open stock market for eighteen to twenty-five times their earnings.

But what about a small company with under $5 million in revenue?

Depending on the industry, you can expect to pay anywhere from two-and-a-half to six times the total annual cash flow to the owner. That's a big range. The large volume of transactions that do not involve a private equity acquisition will settle in at an approximate three to four times.

To apply this knowledge, let's reexamine the example from Chapter 1, where the company was generating $216,000 in annual cash flow. In a business of this size, the cash flow will be calculated by looking at all cash the company is generating for the benefit of the owner. We'll get into the details of this later. For now, just know that it's referred to as seller's discretionary earnings (SDE, or sometimes just "DE" for discretionary earnings).[20] This represents the total pretax cash flow benefit to the owner of the company. In other words, the total amount of cash that can be used for ongoing salary, debt service, reinvestment, etc.

Let's assume that this company can be acquired for 3.2 times the SDE, or $691,200. Let's also assume you'll have an additional $200,000 in inventory and working capital, as well as $50,000 in closing costs and legal fees. This bring the total cash need to $941,200.

You decide to maximize your ROI by reducing your capital infusion as much as possible. You work with an SBA lender to acquire the business with a 10 percent down payment, or $94,120 out of pocket.

When the total benefit is used to calculate the annual ROI to the buyer, it's a staggering 230 percent. The investor invests $94,000 and gets $216,000 as an annual return. Although it's important to understand that just like in real estate or private equity, you need to pay back the bank. In this example, about half your cash flow is now going to equity buildup in the form of monthly debt payments for the acquisition. It's a lot, but not bad considering a 90 percent leveraged asset.

Despite the debt payments, you're still getting just over $100,000 in annual cash flow to either take as salary or reinvest into the company, which translates on its own to an annual ROI of over 100 percent, since it's more than your initial down payment.

---

20 In the middle market, this same number is referred to as Adjusted EBITDA, which stands for Earnings Before Interest, Taxes, Depreciation, and Amortization. It's "adjusted" because it adds back any non-cash expenses, one-time expenses, or direct Owner Benefits, such as salary, benefits, auto expense, and so on.

To put this in perspective, conservative, long term professional investors will attempt to beat the market's historical 8 percent annual ROI.[21] In real estate investing, the rent paid out to the owner in comparison to the purchase price of the building is called the capitalization rate, or "cap rate." Cap rates tend to fluctuate between 4 percent and 12 percent depending on the risk associated with the tenant and other variables. Forbes published an article stating that the average cap rate over a portfolio of real estate should level out to about 9 percent.[22] Here, the analogous cap rate would be 24 percent,[23] or comfortably more than double that of a comparable real estate investment.

Keep in mind that the total realized ROI for the investment will also include the sale of the company when you decide to exit, and not yet included in the calculated 230 percent annual ROI. We'll extrapolate this when we consider upside potential. For now, just understand that the total realized ROI for the investment should exceed the annual ROI.

This investment model wasn't invented by acquisition entrepreneurs. This is exactly the business model driving the entire private equity industry. Doesn't it make sense to apply it to entrepreneurship? Acquisition entrepreneurs simply borrow the business model of private equity rather than that of venture capital.

This is great when it works. However, taking on a lot of debt to buy anything is risky. If it goes wrong you could end up bankrupt,

---

21   By nature, 50 percent fail to achieve this and simply die to the law of averages.

22   https://www.forbes.com/sites/bradthomas/2015/04/22/understanding-cap-rates-the-answer-is-nine/#59a6862e5c32

23   $216,000 in SDE, which is comparable to the "net operating income" of a real estate investment, divided by $891,200, the value of the company ($691,200 purchase price + $200,000 in inventory and working capital).

upside down on your investment, and divorced. Further, selling a privately held company is not quick and easy like a publicly traded stock. It's critical you understand the risks.

The ROI on small business ownership can be great, but just how risky is small business acquisition?

MARGIN OF SAFETY

Risk is relative. The risk-return spectrum dictates that the more risk an investor takes the greater the return needs to be. Unfortunately, the "high risk, high return" model frequently plays out in the high-risk part winning out and producing lower returns.[24]

Warren Buffett, widely considered one of the most successful investors in the world, practices what's called *value investing*. The fundamental belief of value investing is that there is an intrinsic value to every company. This intrinsic value is not an exact number and is subjective in nature. In loose terms, it can be derived by calculating a liquidation value, then observing the additional value a company produces over and above that: competitive advantage, brand awareness, and present value of future cash flows, for example.

Buffet is notorious for investing only in offerings he understands, focusing on tangible assets and earnings, and buying when the price is favorable to its intrinsic value. The built-in assets, infrastructure, and earnings of the company in this case create a *margin of safety* for the investor.

Benjamin Graham and David Dodd, regarded as the inventors of value investing, coined the term *margin of safety* in 1934. It was so fundamental to Graham's thinking that he was quoted as saying, "Confronted with a challenge to distill the secret of sound

---

24 *https://seekingalpha.com/article/4108577-high-risk-high-reward-think*

investment into three words, we venture the motto, *margin of safety.*"

This margin of safety refers to when an investor only purchases securities when the market price is significantly below its intrinsic value.[25] More recently, Warren Buffett and his partner, Charles Munger, made the concept popular by using it to attain extraordinary results.

By investing when the price is favorable to the intrinsic value, it effectively limits the downside risk, building in a level of protection into the investment. Managing the downside risk is one of the great fundamental practices of the world's most famous investors. It's similar to the old adage in real estate, "You make money when you buy, not when you sell." That framework is the anchor for real estate investors the world over.

Many will misunderstand what I just said. They will focus on paying only two-and-a-half times SDE instead of four times on a specific deal. Largely, the market will set the price of any individual investment; and although you shouldn't buy incorrectly, it's more my feeling that the small business private market already trades at its approximate intrinsic value. Perhaps this is because the market is fragmented, so potential buyers can't always find the right sellers. Or perhaps it's because private companies are illiquid and tough to trade if you wish to sell. More likely, the valuations have rightly settled in at a level in which a buyer can acquire them and make an appropriate return.

One way to illustrate the margin of safety in buying a small business compared to other forms of entrepreneurship is by considering how much is at risk and the odds that the company could completely fail.

---

25   *http://www.investopedia.com/terms/m/marginofsafety.asp*

As we've seen, the average startup launches with $65,000 in invested capital and has an approximate 90 percent chance of failure.

A venture-backed firm accepts an average of $41 million per startup and has an approximate 75 percent change of failure. Now let's compare that to the acquisition entrepreneurship model.

Backing into an approximate by reviewing multiple sources, it seems that about 80 percent of small businesses transact for an amount below $1,000,000. Let's use the entire amount of the transaction ($1,000,000) rather than the invested down payment since this encompasses the total risk associated with the acquisition.

According to the Small Business Administration,[26] default rates of small business loans are currently right about 2 percent. Similarly, according to the Thompson Reuters/PayNet Small Business Delinquency Index (SBDI),[27] the amount of small business loans that go delinquent on the national level has been running under 1.5 percent since 2012.

This means the $1 million at risk when acquiring a business has about a 2 percent chance of failure. This is a drastically different profile than building from scratch. If you equate *not failing* with success, then buying a company has an approximate 98 percent success rate.

You could argue this is because small business valuations tend to be closer to their inherent value, rather than the somewhat irresponsible valuations of startups with no revenue, no infrastructure, and no earnings. They take a "what do you need to be a billion-dollar

---

26   https://www.sba.gov/sites/default/files/Finance-FAQ-2016_WEB.pdf

27   https://paynet.com/issues-and-solutions/all-paynet-products/small-business-delinquency-index-sbdi/

company" approach, rather than a valuation based on earnings.

From the point of view of an investor, you can see the asymmetrical risk tied to the different investments and see that there is a margin of safety built in to business acquisition, since the valuation formulas are based on very real past earnings.

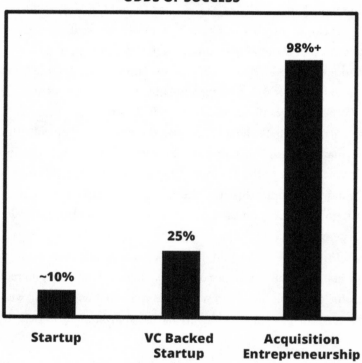

ODDS OF SUCCESS

Figure 2.1: Odds of Success

A company selling at four times its earnings, for example, is conceptually providing a four-year payback to the investor. Conversely, the $41 million in VC money has a 25 percent chance of being paid back at all. There are people who have been very successful in either approach, but if it's engineering success into entrepreneurial efforts that we're after, buying before building might be just the tool we're after, since it eliminates so much of the unnecessary risk associated with entrepreneurship.

In addition, the cost of entry typically isn't much more than that of your average startup because of the debt vehicles you'll have access to. The debt is typically collateralized by the hard assets of the company. So, even though we're using $1,000,000 as the total outstanding risk amount in this illustration, in practice it will be significantly lower.

Like Graham, Dodd, Munger, and Buffet, acquisition entrepreneurs build in a margin of safety, simply by starting with acquiring profitable revenue first, then building from there.

UPSIDE POTENTIAL

Having a margin of safety is critical for protection if the worst would happen, but that's not why we invest. We invest because of the upside potential available in an investment. We've illustrated how a positive ROI can be had in an acquisition, but the upside potential for an acquisition entrepreneur surpasses most investments by a long shot.

Earlier in the chapter, we discussed both cash flow and appreciation as the primary vehicles of driving return on an investment. We bought an asset for $100 and sold it for $120 seven years later. Over the course of the twenty years following 1996, the median residential home sale price appreciated at a rate of 3.1 percent annual compounded rate.[28] Not bad.

However, because acquisition entrepreneurs are active in their business, they can use their time, commitment, and skillset to grow revenue and increase earnings. This is where entrepreneurs have

---

28   Sources: National Association of Realtors, Zillow, The Economist

the advantage over all other investment classes and are really able to hit the acceleration pedal. If you were attempting to increase your appreciated value in real estate, for example, there's not much you can do. The market moves, and the value of the homes move with it. It's not even called "appreciation" in business, it's just called building value. And after you buy, you are going to build.

Perhaps your most critical initiative as an acquisition entrepreneur will be to grow your business. In the four years following March 2013, revenue reported by ultra-small businesses (those generating under $1 million in revenue) increased 20 percent.[29] Revenue is one of the key drivers of business value, and the same report signals a 13.5 percent increase in transaction price over the same time period.

Equity Value at 10% Revenue Growth

Business can grow at 10 percent or more in revenue per year over the prior year. A business with an aggressive growth rate reaps tremendous value increase. If a 10 percent growth rate is achievable in your business, then it will be twice the size it is today in just seven years. The cash flow increases and the value of your asset increases, providing a vehicle for building wealth.

---

29   http://www.bizbuysell.com/news/media_insight.html

Now you're doing something you love, paying yourself, building your team, growing your business, building equity through your debt payments, and reinvesting when needed. Heck, you might even choose to accelerate the growth of your company through additional acquisitions and fund them entirely through the cash flow of your business.

Your business has one thing that no other investment has. You. And *you* are a value creator. Do not wait. Get to work immediately building value.

AN ILLUSTRATION

Let's look at an example scenario so we can walk through what this looks like in practice. It's grossly full of assumptions, but they'll help sketch a blueprint of how it all works, allowing you to see how building value in your business might look.

Let's return to our hypothetical $216,000 in SDE company. You've bought the company for 3.2 times SDE, or $691,200. Then the working capital and inventory added $200,000, and closing costs and lawyer fees were another $50,000. This made the total transaction $941,200.

You put 10 percent down, or $94,120, and took the balance of $847,080 out as an SBA loan at a 6 percent interest rate.[30]

You pay $9,400 in loan payments every month from the $18,000 in available cash flow from the business.[31] This leaves $8,600 in available cash flow to pay yourself and any additional management, or to reinvest into marketing or product development.

You decide you can grow the sales of the business at 10 percent every year during that ten years.

---

30   SBA rates are typically floating at prime plus 2 percent, but for the illustration we'll
     pick a fixed rate of 6 percent for ease.

31   $216,000 in SDE divided by twelve months.

We said this business was generating $1.4 million in annual revenue at the time of purchase. Growing at 10 percent every year, you exceed $2 million in year four and $3 million in year eight. By year ten, your company is generating $3.6 million in annual revenue. Assuming SDE maintains at 15 percent of revenue, the company is now generating $540,000 per year in owner benefit.

And guess what? Your bank loan is paid off, so the $9,400 per month that was going to them is now coming to you. In addition, you've built up the equity in the company. If you did choose to exit the business, the bank is no longer owed any money.

Because you grew the company at a healthy 10 percent every year, you get a higher multiple of SDE when you sell. In year eleven, you agree to exit at a price of four times SDE, which equals $2.2 million. You sell the inventory and working capital to the buyer in addition to the purchase price, so you get an estimated additional $2.5 million at exit.

Not bad for a $94,000 investment. The exit of $2.5 million represents a 35 percent compounded annual interest rate on your original investment. But don't forget you had the benefit of the cash flow and equity build up from the SDE the entire time. Your total pretax compensation from the original $94,000 investment, less the debt payments, is $5,747,934. This represents an astronomical 45 percent compounded annual growth rate.

Just for comparison, the same $94,000 in value invested in real estate would have appreciated to $132,000 in that same eleven years.[32] A balanced stock portfolio generating 8 percent would have increased to $219,000.

---

32 It's an unfair comparison because real estate has a cash flow component as well as equity build up, but the point illustrated here is that the value that can be built in your own privately owned business is not limited like other asset classes.

INVESTMENT	YEAR	REVENUE	SDE	EXIT
$94,120	0	$1,400,000	$210,000	
	1	$1,540,000	$231,000	
	2	$1,694,000	$254,100	
	3	$1,863,400	$279,510	
	4	$2,049,740	$307,461	
	5	$2,254,714	$338,207	
	6	$2,480,185	$372,028	
	7	$2,728,203	$409,230	
	8	$3,001,024	$450,154	
	9	$3,301,127	$495,169	
	10	$3,625,000	$543,750	
	11	$3,987,500	$598,125	$2,500,000
Total Return (less debt payments)				**$5,747,934**

Figure 2.2: Sample Projection

A FASTER ROUTE TO VALUE CREATION

Acquisition entrepreneurship is an active, rather than passive, approach to investing. By aligning your work with your asset, you're able to take wealth building into your own hands and build something worth working for.

It takes a lot of hard work and long hours, but with acquisition comes ownership of something with inherent value from the beginning and puts you in the driver seat for increasing that value. The acquisition entrepreneur is immediately an investor in her company and in herself. With the future under her control, the potential value delivered to the world and the financial upside can be accelerated and significant.

Traditional startups focus entirely on the "appreciation" lever—attempting to create something out of nothing—while starting with acquisition has the same outcome as most successful startups but provides a very bankable asset with a margin of safety and a promising ROI model.

This book builds a roadmap based on the principles that drive a small business transaction from under $1 million up to about $20 million and beyond. That may seem like a big range, but the rules in this segment are all handled essentially the same.

One thing that the venture capital firms are getting wrong is that 99.9 percent of all exits occur with companies under $30 million in revenue—and the trend is increasing. The demand for buying this size firm is approaching insatiable—especially in the technology industry. In Basil Peters' book, *Early Exits: Exit Strategies for Entrepreneurs and Angel Investors (But Maybe Not Venture Capitalists)*, he boasts the demand and benefits of smaller exits. Peters highlights that smaller exits between $15 and $30 million are too small for the press to pick up and an excellent way for the entrepreneur and angel investor to make several million dollars at exit.

Larger companies don't innovate from scratch anymore; they are just too big. Google, for example, did not even invent Adsense—their enormous pay per click management platform—they acquired Adscape for $23 million and built it out from there.

Smaller exits, defined as those under $30 million, are where all the action is and exactly where you won't find VCs. More and more private equity firms have figured this out, but in companies with less than $2 million in earnings, even they begin to be noticeably absent. Smaller exits and smaller acquisitions are the realm of the acquisition entrepreneur—and exactly the area where they can make millions.

All that said, let me be clear that although entrepreneurs have a wonderful vehicle for engineering long-term wealth in their companies, they are almost never driven by wealth creation. Entrepreneurs have non-financial benefits that drive them. We relish in the autonomy, problem solving, growth, and passion we have for our companies. These aspects are not lacking in the acquisition model. For a true entrepreneur, financial independence has been reached the moment they take ownership of a company or an idea, from the very beginning, because there is no separation between work and life. It is the same mission and the same time. This is because for an entrepreneur, working hard for something they care deeply about is the life worth living. It's fun, and these benefits are attainable on day one. Perhaps this is the "real" wealth we all want—the purpose that comes along with creating value in your life.

So who are these entrepreneurs? What does it take to succeed? What drives them? And how can we know whether we are built from that cloth? These are the questions we address in the next chapter.

PART 2

EVALUATION

"Set your mind on a definite goal and observe how quickly the world stands aside to let you pass."

—NAPOLEON HILL

CHAPTER 3

THE CEO MINDSET

MOST PEOPLE START LOOKING FOR A COMPANY TO ACQUIRE completely the wrong way. They start by thinking about what industry they would like to target. Even most intermediaries start with this question: what type of business do you want to find? Rarely is this the right place to begin. With the exception of a definitive motivation to stay in the same industry to leverage existing relationships or unique operational advantage toward a specific opportunity, this is completely backwards.

Successful acquisition entrepreneurs turn the traditional search process upside down. They understand correctly that the building blocks of how to build a company and a vision don't come from what's "on the menu," but from aligning their attitude, aptitude, and action, and leveraging that alignment toward a specific opportunity.

Knowing *why and how you will win* before you start is critical to knowing what game you are looking for in the first place.

Starting with yourself, and aligning your "3 As" of attitude, aptitude, and action, will help identify the right parameters for your search. Aligning all three of these will allow you to move forward with conviction. Without them, you either waste people's time or risk failure. Or both. To find the right acquisition for you, it's exactly that—the right acquisition *for you*. So, start with yourself. The rest will come together later. Trust the process.

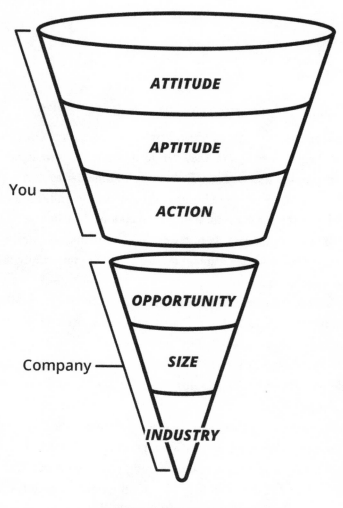

Target Statement

BUILDING BLOCKS

I have found the best way to understand successful people is by looking at the research. What does it take to run a successful company? What is the skillset needed? Are these skills innate or can they be learned? These are the questions that budding entrepreneurs start to ask when they learn that the acquisition model skips the startup phase and goes right to running a successful company from day one.

Look at the list below. These include some of the most recognized character traits of successful CEOs in companies between $1 and $20 million in revenue. A few of them *seem* like they would be characteristics of strong entrepreneurs, but they actually are not. As you read through it, consider how strongly you see each attribute in yourself and what traits might be missing. Also consider what might be missing from the list.

- Strategic-thinking skills
- Interpersonal skills
- Intellectual ability
- Industry experience
- Ability to deal with ambiguity
- Tenacity
- Organized
- Laser-focused
- Achievement-oriented
- Thick-skinned
- Risk tolerant
- Self-confident
- Creative
- Optimistic

- Assertive
- Decisive
- Methodical
- Perfectionistic

Got it? Before reviewing the results, I want you to understand that data suggests that the number one characteristic of being successful is not on this list at all. It's not a skill we would see in a job description or resume. Instead of looking at how we work and what we do, the key to success is in *how we think*.

The first step toward being a successful leader of your own company is to *think* like a CEO in the first place. If you don't cultivate the "right" thoughts, you're defeated before you start. You need to eventually build a vision of where you are headed and how you will get there, but without the mental wherewithal to navigate the waters, it's just a business plan.

After significant research into what makes successful entrepreneurs, I've come to think of them as a three-legged stool—they require all three legs to function, and without any one of them, the stool falls. For the acquisition entrepreneur to find the *right* company and have success running it, they too need to have all three attributes working in harmony: Attitude, Aptitude, and Action. This is the *Law of Three As* mentioned earlier.

ATTITUDE

Successful entrepreneurs all have something in common. One of the most tremendous predictors of long-term success is having a *growth mindset*. Carol Dweck, a world-renowned Stanford University psychologist and the author of *Mindset: How We Can Learn to Fulfill Our Potential*, has become the world's leading expert on the growth mindset—both how to identify it and how to cultivate it in yourself and your children.

Dweck makes a distinction between a growth mindset and a fixed mindset. A fixed mindset is one that thinks in terms of absolutes, such as, "This is the way things are, and this is the way they will always be." People with fixed mindsets have core beliefs that reflect it. They believe in limited resources; they believe that people have an innate and fixed level of intelligence and that effortless success is the badge of the truly talented. If someone has to put forth enormous effort, it reflects a lack of skill or talent. It means that effort is a bad thing and reflects that a person is not smart or talented.

Fixed mindsets believe that the qualities of a person are carved in stone—permanent. They need to constantly prove themselves to confirm their character or intelligence. They worry about how they are received and are typically more risk averse because, if they fail, they perceive *themselves* as "a failure." In a 2016 article for the *Harvard Business Review*, Dweck summarized a fixed mindset as being held by those who believe their talents are innate gifts and worry about looking smart.[33]

On the contrary, a growth mindset is one that views the world as more malleable, believing success is achieved through effort. A growth mindset is the little difference that empowers people to have a sense of free will. They embrace rather than avoid challenge, and they persist during times of setback. A growth mindset views effort as the path to mastery. They learn from criticism and are inspired by the success of others. Hard work, good strategies, and input from others are the tools utilized by those who believe their talents can be developed. They put their energy into learning.

---

33 Carol Dweck, *What Having a "Growth Mindset" Actually Means, Harvard Business Review*, January, 2016.

Growth-minded people seem to take the attitude, "Anything can be improved upon, and I'm the one to do it." Ultimately, it's the ability to learn from your experiences and not make the same mistakes repeatedly. As a result, all the empirical evidence suggests that people that have cultivated a growth mindset reach ever-increasing levels of achievement. Indeed, Dweck's research has supported the hypothesis that people who favor and deliberately practice a growth mindset tend to achieve more than those with a more fixed mindset.

Having a growth mindset is an enormous psychological advantage for those who have it. The knowledge that things are malleable creates an interest for solving market problems, generating innovative solutions, and implementing ongoing improvement—both for yourself and your work—which is the mark of successful entrepreneur. A fixed mindset, by contrast, confirms a deterministic view of the world and results in never achieving your full potential.

Without a growth mindset, Elon Musk's SpaceX would never have achieved successful trips to the International Space Station after the first three rockets literally crashed and burned. Or, take Thomas Edison. His teachers notoriously said he was "too stupid to learn anything," and he ultimately failed over 1,000 times before eventually creating the lightbulb. Both of these people show grit and determination, but ultimately the belief that the solution can eventually be reached by a series of smaller improvements. These are enormous and tremendously expensive examples from iconoclastic entrepreneurs—but that's exactly the point. Most of this book has covered building a margin of safety into entrepreneurship, but the growth mindset points to the tremendous upside potential of an opportunity.

The good news is if you aren't currently oriented toward a growth mindset, it can be cultivated. Dweck observed that everyone is a mix of growth and fixed mindsets. Changing your thoughts toward developing a dominant growth-oriented mindset is the first step to becoming a CEO. Dweck advises that the first step in the path of change is identifying when your thoughts take on a fixed framework. She suggests we learn our fixed mindset "voice." This voice appears in our thoughts during times of challenge, setbacks, or when facing criticism. If your thoughts revolve around fearing failure, risk, or blaming others rather than taking responsibility, then you may want to spend some time getting your mindset ready for the job.

After identifying when you're having fixed mindset thoughts, Dweck suggests the next steps are to recognize that you have a choice in how you interpret the challenge, setbacks, or criticism; then "talk back" to the fixed voice with a growth mindset voice. Examples she gives are, "If I don't try, I automatically fail"; "Others who succeeded before me had passion and put forth effort"; and, "If I don't take responsibility, I can't fix it."

Finally, take on the challenge, learn from your struggle, and try again.

Dweck has concluded that organizations have a collective mindset as well. Growth mindset companies enjoy feelings of empowerment and commitment by employees, as well as a far greater support for collaboration and innovation. Fixed mindset environments tend to cultivate cheating and deception. Sure, these are extreme examples, but some mild reflection will remind you of various places you may have worked and where they fall on the spectrum. We all know that entrepreneurs define the culture of the company, so how you think will be reflected in every aspect around you.

Having a growth mindset is often regarded as the number one predictor of entrepreneurial success. It allows a leader to learn from their mistakes and adapt. Knowing that there is always risk that needs to be managed, that rough waters can be successfully navigated, and having an almost relentless commitment to ongoing improvement is what separates the growth-minded entrepreneur from the pack.

In acquisition entrepreneurship the stakes are high, and having the right attitude can be the difference between making it happen or sitting on the bench missing opportunities. Cultivating the right attitude by increasing your growth mindset and aligning your personal mission with Seligman's PERMA formula is the key to unlocking success, both now and after you acquire a company.

APTITUDE

Aptitude is made up of both raw intelligence and competencies. These are your skillsets, your strengths and weaknesses.

Raw intellect has been measured by IQ tests for decades. As a result, we have a lot of data around IQ and its correlation with successful businesses results. High intellectual ability is currently the single largest predictor of success in entrepreneurship and in management. In fact, high IQ plus the drive to succeed is the essential formula for success.[34]

In sharp contrast to our last section, it is important to highlight that raw intellect, by the time we are adults, is completely fixed. Working extremely hard to improve your IQ doesn't really move the needle. And although there is a correlation to increasing IQ levels and years in school, you have to wonder whether people who keep getting additional schooling clearly resonate with school in the first place.

---

34 Chad H. Van Iddekinge, Herman Aguinis, Jeremy D. Mackey, Philip S. DeOrtentiis, "A Meta-Analysis of the Interactive, Additive, and Relative Effects of Cognitive Ability and Motivation on Performance" *Journal of Management*, January, 2018.

That said, there is lots good news but if you find yourself, like most of humanity, somewhere in the middle of the intelligence bell curve, do not fear. First, many understand that IQ has had a dominating run over the course of decades as the leading attribute to assess. Many believe, and emerging data supports, that Emotional Intelligence, or "EQ," will trend its way beyond IQ as the leading driver of performance. Second, many of the other leading competencies are not as innate and can be learned. So even if you already have them in spades, there are opportunities to improve and design yourself into the CEO you want to be.

Let's review the list from the beginning of the chapter.

As promised, I slipped some false positives in there. At first glance, it would appear that being organized, methodical, and laser-focused seems like it would be a great characteristic of a successful entrepreneur. The truth is that there is no correlation between having strong organizational skills and a successful CEO. None.

In business, ambiguity reigns. Being laser-focused is actually a bad thing. Entrepreneurs need to be able to deal with managing *ambiguity* and a changing landscape; the best ones do this extremely well. In 2003, I was in business school. My professor asked us to cut a piece of paper into eight pieces, then write the following words, one on each piece: sales, marketing, financial measures, competition, process, suppliers, incentives. Then he instructed us to mix them up, then randomly remove half and throw them away. "In real life, business looks more like the paper left in your hand—you don't have all the information when it's decision time." It's an academic exercise, but illustrative of the ambiguity innate to running a business.

At first glance, creativity is something that would appear to be good during an early startup but perhaps require "adult supervision" later. Actually, creativity, although rare in most small business management, is one of the traits that separates the wheat from the chaff in this line of work. Getting creative about how to solve problems can separate your company from others and add incredible value to your customers. Creativity isn't restricted to product innovation, it includes the decisions made every day inside an organization.

Above all, strategic thinking, persistence, assertiveness, and being achievement-oriented, optimistic, and thick-skinned are the attributes most shared by successful entrepreneurs. That said, most small business owners tend to be very tactical, not strategic at all. If you are tactical, this can be good news, while those who think more strategically, will see benefits in operating at a different level.

Being decisive and self-confident is important up to a certain extent, but too much results in approaching cockiness and overestimating your own capabilities, which is a clear negative according to the empirical evidence.

Perfectionism, as well, is a negative. In entrepreneurship, *action* is rewarded over perfection. Extreme attention to detail tends to keep action at bay indefinitely, or at least results in delayed implementation.

Entrepreneurship is almost synonymous with a high-risk tolerance. It's one of the first things people think of when startups are mentioned. Indeed, people who have a tolerance for risky endeavors will eventually find themselves participating in all-or-nothing type activities, and the startup model emulates the high risk-high return profile. That said, most startups fail, and the ones with high risk tolerance tend to fall in that category. Successful entrepreneurs tend to consider themselves comfortable with a certain amount of risk, but are extremely calculated in their efforts. We can't go so far to claim that entrepreneurs are risk *averse* because practicing business has a certain level of risk associated by nature—debt financing and decision making with limited information, for example—but many entrepreneurs actually consider themselves risk averse, despite the reputations they hold publicly. Acquisition entrepreneurship, of course, is an example of how I have limited my own risk exposure.

While evaluating yourself on this list, understand that most people think they are better than they actually are when assessing their own strengths and weaknesses, while top performers are tough on themselves.[35] I always recommend hiring a professional company to assess you for this reason, as they can help bring you clarity in this area. The next best tactic is to enlist the help of some friends and colleagues when embarking on a self-assessment. After assessing yourself, show the list above to your spouse or a good friend. What skills do they feel you possess? This will be powerful feedback—try to just listen.

A common question is, once we have a sense of our strengths and weaknesses, how do we measure the *relative* strength of the attributes we *do* have? A recent interview with Dr. David Weller, founder of Leadership Alliance and a true expert in assessing top talent, told me that about a third of the variants for success are simple competencies. These include, but are not limited to:

- Possessing a drive for results and being able to get results from others
- The ability to make decisions, including unpopular decisions
- Strategic agility when dealing with ambiguity
- A certain level of risk tolerance
- Financial acumen

---

35 David Dunning, Chip Heath, and Jerry M. Suls, "Flawed Self-Assessment, Implications for Health, Education, and the Workplace," *American Psychological Society*, 2004. Psychological Science in the Public Interest.

- Critical thinking, which is an innate trait
- Tactical ability
- Perseverance
- Self-awareness, which includes the ability to work through your weaknesses and not have blind spots
- Interpersonal skills

The last one is worth noting. When you are CEO of a company, you must be able to sell; it's a requirement. This does not mean that you need to commit your time to being a salesperson—that will depend on the type of opportunity you choose. The ability to grow small companies into big companies will always include the skill of *selling*, which is a learnable skill, despite the thought that salespeople are either born with this talent or not. Whether you're selling your services to a prospective customer, selling the vision of your company to the employees, or selling the model to a potential investor, sales skills are a fundamental requirement of growing a business. Having strong interpersonal skills makes it possible to connect people and activities and grow a business.

In 2002, the *Journal of Business Venturing* published a study[36] that established ten behavioral areas of competence for entrepreneurs that have either a direct or an indirect impact on performance.

- Analytical
- Innovative
- Operational
- Human

---

36 Lau T. Man and K.F. Chan, (2002), "The competitiveness of small and medium enterprises. A conceptualization with focus on entrepreneurial competencies," *Journal of Business Venturing*, 17:2, pp. 123–42.

- Strategic
- Opportunity
- Relationship
- Commitment
- Learning
- Personal Growth

Obviously, not all successful entrepreneurs have all of these traits at the same level, and some may even lack a trait or two completely, but overall, getting the recipe right with these ingredients is what all the empirical evidence suggests is the winner. Essentially, getting a *resourceful and driven individual committed to a good opportunity* will win *every* time.

PERMA

Positive psychology is the scientific study of human flourishing. No kidding. Martin Seligman is currently the Director of the Penn Positive Psychology Center and Zellerbach Professor of Psychology at the University of Pennsylvania. When he was voted President of the American Psychological Association in 1998, he essentially invented and promoted the study of positive psychology. He's authored numerous books on the subject.

Seligman first started studying what became positive psychology while working with one of the biggest insurance companies in the world to help them discover the differences in sales people who had tremendous success versus those who quickly burned out. The goal was to find a way to make better hires.

His research discovered that *optimism* was the common characteristic among successful salespeople within the agency. In one of his more recent books, *Flourish: A Visionary New Understanding of*

Happiness and Well-Being, he reveals the five pillars of well-being, which he identified through the acronym PERMA:

- Positive emotion
- Engagement
- Relationships
- Meaning
- Achievement

PERMA is a five-pillar list of ingredients, but the recipe for living the best life possible is different for every individual. Some people require a greater *meaning* in their lives, while others focus on *engaging* work or nurturing *relationships*. Achievement means just that—people driven by *achievement* in their lives in order to truly flourish as individuals.

Most entrepreneurs are highly achievement-driven. Psychologist Henry Murray devised a characteristic that he called "the need to achieve," which refers to an individual's desire for significant accomplishment: intense, prolonged, and repeated efforts to accomplish something difficult. To many highly driven people, achievement is oftentimes more important than financial reward or receiving praise or recognition. Financial reward is viewed as a measure of success, but not an end to itself. Those who are dubbed "high achievers" are those who are motivated almost exclusively by the personal satisfaction that comes with accomplishing hard goals.

It's clear that achievement is essential for entrepreneurs to live as their fullest and best selves. This achievement is the likely driver for our motivation, our commitment, and our persistence. Being achievement-oriented plays very well with the entrepreneur. If this doesn't resonate with you, really ask yourself why you want to run a business.

We covered the importance of the growth mindset as an indicator of success in your life, but understanding PERMA aligns you with what you should focus on.

As a CEO, be calculated, be resourceful, and be persistent. These are the winning competencies of entrepreneurs the world over.

ACTION

Imagine your perfect work day. What are your doing with your time? What *drives* you? This is the *engagement* pillar in Seligman's PERMA recipe. What activities are you doing when you become completely engaged, lose track of time, or enjoy yourself the most? This is your "right action." Having a firm understanding of what you want your daily activities to look like will help you identify the right opportunity later.

Most business activities are typically divided into two core, overarching functions. One side of the spectrum is revenue generation and the other is operational execution. Are you a *grow the top line*-oriented individual or are you interested in *operational execution*? In other words, do you want to sell more product, or make as much product as possible at the lowest cost? Everyone has a natural inclination toward one side or the other. If you are considering acquisition entrepreneurship, you will need to be able to function on *both sides* of this spectrum.

Sales/Marketing	**Operations/Accounting**
(Revenue Generation)	(Profit Management)

However, every potential acquisition worth being considered comes with a built-in opportunity. You need to know whether you are growth-oriented or operationally oriented. Moreover, you need to acquire a business where the execution of the opportunity for increasing value matches not only your skillset but aligns with your vision of what you want to do on a daily basis.

Some believe firmly that this activity should be what you've done before, something you have a track record of. I find this isn't always the case, since it depends on which path your career has taken up to this point. The best leaders will know where they are strong and where they will hire—regardless of past roles. Some want to accelerate the activities they've done before in an acquisition while others what to change what they are doing. You'll find either option is available to you, so deciding now will guide your "true north" during the search process.

Gino Wickman, author of *Traction: Get a Grip on Your Business* and life-long entrepreneur, outlines two types of business owners: visionaries or integrators. His concept is similar to the revenue or operations spectrum we've presented here. He sees the visionary as the entrepreneurs who are able to see into the future. They can take an idea and run sixty miles an hour down the street until it sticks. The integrators pick up the pieces that have been left in the wake of the visionary, organize, and profitably execute. Ideally, every organization would have one of each, and in smaller businesses, usually that's you—until you are able to grow or scale to a different level.

Whether it's the visionary or the operator executing the sales and marketing activities, growth is going to be a key function in building value in your organization. Take time to define how that growth should be executed. Is it consumer marketing? Direct sales? Online ads or expanding existing customer relationships? You can identify which of these your skillset aligns with the most without looking at a single acquisition opportunity, and you need to know the answer so you can understand when you see the right fit.

Before you start looking for a company, it's critical you take the time to outline your vision for the future. This outline starts with a deep dive into yourself.

Make a list of all of your career accomplishments to date and what behaviors drove those results. Being immediately in touch with your successes will become important down the road when you talk with bankers as well. For now, consider what challenges you have overcome. What have you committed yourself to and achieved exceptional results with?

What activities do you enjoy actually doing? Do you enjoy coordinating lots of people's activities? Digging into metrics? Calling on big accounts? Solving problems? Those are all great, high-level descriptions, but what about the details? Do you enjoy talking on the phone or managing emails all day? Running daily production meetings? Keeping the accounting tight? Going on sales calls? Managing the depths of an online marketing campaign? Integrating new systems into an organization?

At the end of this exercise, you should have a clear idea of what specific actions you want to be performing in your daily role.

PERSONAL SWOT

SWOT, a common business strategy practice, flushes out the strengths, weaknesses, opportunities, and threats of a particular business. Applying this common business strategy to yourself will fine-tune your self-understanding.

The strengths you identified in the last section can go under your strengths, but what about your weaknesses? Just as important as knowing what you're good at and what you enjoy is knowing what type of activities you should avoid. What areas, tasks, and even possible industries are off limits for you? What activities just absolutely do not interest you? What assignments do you drag your feet on? These should be identified so you can concentrate on working within your sweet spot and focus on what you do best. Get it all down on paper: the good, the bad, and the ugly.

Once you've examined where you thrive and what to avoid, it's time to build your resume. The exercise of putting it together is an important part of looking inward. Record your relevant work experience and what your role was in each position. Be sure to use action verbs to frame your accomplishments; quantify the specific results you achieved. This helps to emphasize what really stands out in your career, where your interests lie, and where and how you get the best results. It also serves to identify what your role should be moving forward. Do you excel in marketing, sales, process implementation, or accounting? What areas are you comfortable growing into and which ones do you want to hire assistance for.

One of the most fatal mistakes an entrepreneur can make is assuming that just because they understand the technical work of the business does not mean they can successfully run a business that does the technical work. As Michael Gerber describes at length in his book *The E-Myth: Why Most Small Businesses Don't Work and What to Do About It*, staffing, marketing, and cash flow management have nothing to do with baking pies, but everything to do with running and growing a pie *business*.

Spend time reflecting on yourself. The exercise will drive interest in opportunities that may have otherwise not appeared interesting. For the purpose of true self-discovery, ignore your passions and interests for a moment. Simply focus on the activities and functions you are well-equipped to execute. This is about getting in tune with what you're good at and doing a deep dive into your skillset. At the end of this section, you should have a personal SWOT analysis and a resume written out for your review.

THE RIGHT PROCESS

By starting with identifying your 3 As of Attitude, Aptitude, and Action, you'll have the groundwork done to move forward with the most success possible. Having insight into what makes a successful entrepreneur and how you line up as well will assist in giving you confidence, highlighting the areas where you need to improve or find a partner, and applying the insights about yourself toward the external component of the company you will lead.

You will find there are good, scalable businesses out there, as well as not so good businesses. But objective evaluation of an opportunity shouldn't begin until you know whether the company profile fits with your goals and skillsets.

Clearly identifying what motivates you, your natural strengths and weaknesses, as well as what you want to actually be doing on a daily basis are all critically more important than what the business does or the opportunity it has. Together, the 3 As provide a framework for knowing where you will thrive, and because of that, what you are looking for in the first place.

In the next chapter, we'll begin to explore how to apply your work on the 3 As to identify the right company for you.

CHAPTER 4

DEFINING THE TARGET

IN THE LAST CHAPTER, WE COVERED THE FIRST THING POTENTIAL buyers need to do: evaluate and align the right Attitude, Aptitude, and Action. This is a critical step. By making a commitment to finding a business in a limited timeframe, defining your strengths, and identifying the activities you want to actually be doing on a daily basis, we're able to lay the proper foundation for a search that will end with a good business that fits you, rather than the other way around.

This chapter will take you from having those insights about yourself to actually outlining what the target company will look like. The way we do this is, first, by identifying the opportunity profile you are looking for, then defining the size of the target company within a range as well as the industry type. We'll also bring into consideration any limiters you might have. That is, variables that immediately rule out a company that you would consider.

Finally, we'll bring it all together into your own personalized *target statement*. Your target statement will be the driver of your search and ascertain that you are communicating exactly what you are looking for to the right people.

OPPORTUNITY PROFILES

The number one thing that I stress when helping people find the right company for them is to match the opportunity profile of the business to their personal strengths and goals. This is why the exercises in the last chapter were so critical. They give you insight about yourself and what you want in a company.

I believe that there are four main models of building value in a company after you acquire it. Although I personally tend to look for more-or-less stable, evergreen businesses with strong potential upside, there are other models to consider based on your strengths. Many buyers I talk with wouldn't even consider a business unless it was a complete mess. Is that you? Maybe you're looking for a turnaround. What about high growth or an "eternally profitable" business? Or perhaps something that has components that allow you to leverage existing relationships for growth? These are all very different profiles, and each is extremely valid.

Although this model is not intended to be exhaustive, I find that most growth opportunities can be mapped into four quadrants by segmenting them in the same way stocks might be: either as a growth or value opportunity.

Let's review them one at a time.

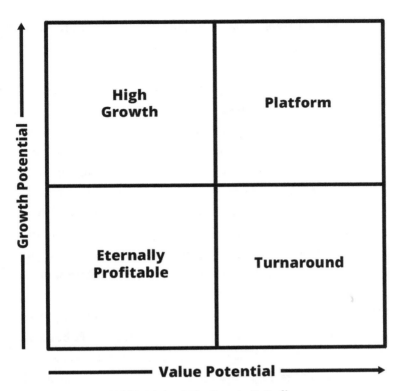

Exhibit 4.1: Acquisition Opportunity Profiles

ETERNALLY PROFITABLE

Richard Ruback and Royce Yudkoff are two Harvard professors who wrote a book called *HBR Guide to Buying a Small Business.* Their preference is to look for what they call "eternally profitable" businesses to acquire. This is the business that serves a need that is very unlikely to go away.

One example of this type of business was profiled in the *New York Times.* In March 2016, the article, "You've Bought a Business. Now What?" profiled the move of three former venture capitalists buying a company for themselves. The article underscored that since they were VCs, it would be fair to assume they would acquire a high-tech company or an online innovator. Instead, the group bought a snow removal and landscaping company.

Snow plowing is an industry that is already mature in nature, so a high-growth future is unlikely. This is a business that might grow their customer list by 1 percent a year. However, because of the extensive infrastructure in roads and automobiles, and the eternal threat of mother nature, snow plowing does not face any significant technological threats either. Even self-driving vehicles need clean roads.

In the same vein, snow removal is a very geographically driven business. You have to actually be in the physical area to service the customers. As long as service is good, customers are unlikely to switch—which means that new entrants into the market are unlikely.

This is exactly the profile of an *eternally profitable* business. It's a "cash cow" with very small growth opportunity, but also small threat of industry disruption. It's a stable and dependable business that you can count on. It may also be assumed from a business like this that the customer relationships have been long established and the company has a dependable track record. By offering landscaping as well, they likely have a way to stay in communication with their customers, as well as invoice year-round.

John Warrillow's book, *The Automatic Customer*, calls for companies to turn to subscription models in order to increase the dependability of revenue and, in turn, the value of their business. This is the same underlying principle that is behind an eternally profitable business—a sort of "software as a service" subscription model.

But it's not necessarily limited to companies with recurring monthly income either. Plumbing, laundry, electricity, boat docks, FBOs, and preschools are all potential examples of business models holding similar "eternal" characteristics.

It's tougher to have a differentiated value proposition in these markets, and they often heavily compete on price, so you'll want to consider what the driver of the business is. The potential drawback to eternally profitable businesses is that companies that sometimes look like they are running in mature markets may actually be in over-fragmented industries ripe for consolidation.

As a high school student in the early 1990s, it was clear that the retail film processing business was a seemingly secure $4.5 billion industry.[37] A good candidate, perhaps, for someone seeking an eternally profitable business. Unfortunately for the owners of those companies, digital photography hit new quality levels and by the end of the decade was widespread. The industry went the way of the buggy-whip, and the largest providers were able to hang on until the mid-2000s.

Disruption is a risk in any business, and the eternally profitable profile takes great care to favor safety from disruption over growth. However, these types of businesses typically provide healthy economics for a consolidation play. But let's not get ahead of ourselves. There will be more on business strategy and evaluating opportunities later. The point is only to highlight the benefits and drawbacks of the eternally profitable model.

TURNAROUND

The turnaround is a tremendous place to create value if you are strong in operations and have a great understanding of financial reports and managing cash flow.

A turnaround describes the acquisition of a company that has fallen on hard times, with the goal of improving operations,

---

37   https://tedium.co/2017/06/01/photo-processing-history-mainstream-phenomenon/

building efficiencies, and strengthening the value that the company provides to its customers. It's the company version of the "fixer-upper." Often, however, the best opportunities are with companies in pretty bad shape, even bankrupt.

Typically, a turnaround opportunity is not valued on positive earnings because they're usually not producing positive earnings. Instead, book value, liquidation value, or some similar metric applies a discount into the more typical, positive-earnings-multiplied formula. I have seen deals where taking over the debt for the opportunity to turn the company around is a horrible idea because they owe too much, and I have also seen where the debt is comfortable under the liquidation value.

These companies typically have complicated messes to work out. Still, for the operational expert, these opportunities can be the diamond in the rough. To them, the assets are acquired for a favorable price and then "fixed." The point is that the assets of the company are discounted from a typical selling valuation— sometimes as low as liquidation value—due to the underperformance of the company.

In August 2017, the *Wall Street Journal* reported on the spectacular turnaround performance of the publicly traded weight loss company Nutrisystem Inc. In 2012, Dawn Zier joined as President and CEO at a time when the company had experienced several years of profit and sales declines. During her efforts, annual profit quadrupled, share value rose 700 percent, and sales increased for sixteen consecutive quarters.

This is a perfect example of how a turnaround can work. This extremely high growth has created tremendous value for the company's customers and shareholders alike. The secret is typically reengineering how things are done within a company and comes with a lot of hard decisions and heartache. Overhead usually needs to be reduced right away, which can mean terminating employees on day one.

In a turnaround, the fundamentals are going to include a good product market fit and ongoing demand in the marketplace for what the company currently produces. The upside potential lives in the operational improvements of a turnaround opportunity, while the risks are usually limited to the ability to execute, something Zier did tremendously well.

HIGH GROWTH

Growth in revenue and earnings is what drives maximum value of every business at the end of the day. A company coming off, say, three years of significant revenue growth is exciting and attractive for many buyers. After all, these are the types of companies making the current owners healthy sums of money.

The good news behind high growth is that there is clearly demand for the product or service, and the company is doing well at delivering it. The bad news is that because revenue and earnings growth drive value, you will be paying more for that prior performance. This is worth it as long as the growth rate continues under your leadership, but paying a higher multiple introduces added risk to your company if you use significant debt in the acquisition process.

This is because the monthly debt service payments will become an overhead expense—something you have to pay every month no matter what happens. If you pay a high multiple of earnings on additional growth that doesn't materialize, you could end up paying too much for the company. Remember the margin of safety we discussed in Chapter 2? Overpaying for a company reduces that margin of safety.

In addition, high-revenue growth typically translates into tight cash flow. This is because the capital earned by the company every month needs to be reinvested in order to keep up with the growth. Whether this is in added infrastructure or inventory, there is typically a growth in expenses to support the growing demand. This will increase your need for additional working capital.

The result is that high-growth acquisitions almost have two risks: if the growth doesn't continue, you risk overpaying for the investment and stressing the cash flow. On the flip side, if the company does continue to grow rapidly, the demand for increased amounts of working capital could also stress cash flow. Either one might require more cash infusion.

In May 2001, the *Harvard Business Review* published an article by Neil Churchill and John Mullins, titled "How Fast Can Your Company Afford to Grow?" In it, the authors guide the reader through evaluating the operating cash cycle and explain how best to manipulate it when needed. They walk you through how understanding the length of time your cash is tied up in the cycle dictates how fast your company can grow without requiring more cash.

It's a complicated exercise to perform, but it has proven to be very valuable. I have repeatedly applied it before acquiring a firm so that I can intimately understand the company's cash cycle and the demands of each cycle. Another great help is to ask for income statements on a cash basis versus an accrual basis for high-growth companies. This will give you insight into the variance in demand for inventory or costs of goods sold per month—a very helpful characteristic to analyze when looking into a high-growth firm.

I had a manufacturing company that I ran this analysis on before I purchased, and the exercise revealed that the company could grow about 42 percent year-over-year before it would need additional cash infused into the company. This is huge growth for a manufacturing company, so it didn't worry me. Eighteen months later, and thanks to a very high performing team, the company had grown over 35 percent over the prior twelve months, which was obviously fantastic. The problem was that this occurred through big projects with big companies. This required more inventory and longer cycle times, which squeezed cash and required additional capital to fund the growth. In business, these are referred to as "happy problems," but needing additional cash to run your business is a problem that could be detrimental to the company's reputation if not fulfilled.

High-growth companies can prove to be good investments and a lot of fun. However, they introduce risk by increasing the variance in results and typically come with an increased price as well because growth increases value. It's essentially the opposite of a turnaround. Instead of the added risk of a company in trouble, it's the added risk of a company in high demand.

PLATFORM

In private equity, a platform company refers to the first company a firm acquires in a specific industry. This is their entrance into that industry and they refer to it as a platform because they intend to grow it. Typically, they would begin to cut expenses, raise prices, and begin an organic growth model of one kind or another. From there, they may acquire other firms in the industry, either as an add-on or tuck-in to the platform they established.

I apply the term platform in a similar fashion here. In acquisition entrepreneurship, a platform company is one where the buyer of the company is typically the one who will be operating within the company themselves as the CEO. As you've seen, I've made you spend time on identifying what you will bring to the table for this company, using your strengths, goals, and interests to match to a specific value-building activity.

While working through the 3 As, you identified whether you want to buy a company to increase value though marketing, organic sales, or by implementing operational excellence. The platform, ideally, would have all of these opportunities for you, similar to what a private equity firm looks for; however, the main driver that identifies a platform is that the specific growth opportunity matches your aptitude and activity goals.

Like the high growth and turnaround profiles, the platform company is defined by the opportunity to create value through your unique skills and motivation.[38] In this case, it addresses the question, "How will you grow it?"

If you have experience in business-to-business sales and know this is where you thrive, finding a well-run, operationally fit company that is lacking a strong sales front might be exactly what you are looking for.

If you have insight into an industry and want to build a SAAS-model software for a certain industry, you can find a company with a customer base ideal for such a rollout.

If you are an operational expert, you may wish to find an opportunity with solid marketing efforts in place, but that lacks efficiency in processes and has obvious needed areas of improvement in quality assurance. You're obviously looking for something where you can roll your sleeves up and start improving the company from the bottom line up.

Or, if you are an online marketing expert, there are plenty of well-established companies out there that sell products successfully through traditional channels that have, so far, ignored online sales efforts. This could be a perfect fit for your skillset.

---

38 An eternally profitable profile is perhaps defined as the opposite—maximizing stability and risk management.

Applying your specific desired growth opportunity to defining the target company you are looking for is the single best way to structure a search. This way, you know what you are looking for and can be comfortable moving forward with conviction when you find it.

A platform company could have any kind of profile. It could be an eternally profitable, high growth, or turnaround. More likely, it's somewhere in the middle. A nice, "good" company with some aspects of stability and some of risk, but the goal is to define an acquisition target by the growth opportunity it provides.

It's a little understood fact that Elon Musk bought PayPal when his own similar startup *X.com*, well, failed. Peter Thiel came with the acquisition and later ran PayPal as CEO. Tesla, as well. Although he is now considered a founder, the company was started by two others and grown very effectively by Musk.

Gary Vaynerchuk took over his parents' liquor store. Seeing an opportunity to sell wine online took revenues from $3 million to $60 million by applying his online marketing skillset to the unique opportunity offered to him by the platform that was available.

Warby Parker's cofounder Jeff Raider, along with Andy Katz-Mayfield, cofounded subscription based shaving startup Harry's by raising enough money to acquire a $100 million razor manufacturing company in Germany,[39] then leveraging their past experience in growing the company online. Today, Harry's is estimated to be generating $70 million in annual revenue.

These are just a couple examples to show that acquiring a company in order to execute on a specific market opportunity works not just for those looking to acquire a business between $500,000 and

---

39 *https://www.inc.com/magazine/201605/bernhard-warner/harrys-razors-german-factory.html*

$5,000,000 in revenue. This model is at work at the highest levels of innovation as well.

However, I don't want to paint a portrait of the platform model serving only toward super-aggressive growth. Most of the time, in practice it's simply the platform for incremental growth. Less than that of a high-growth company, but more than that of an eternally profitable one. A good goal would be a 10 percent year-over-year pace.

Each of these examples defined the target company by the growth opportunity they wanted to execute over any other variable. This is the driver behind the platform profile.

LOOKING FOR GROWTH

Whenever I am looking at any business, I'm looking to identify the path to growth and the amount of upside potential. How big can this business be? Try to understand the driver behind a company's value and how to best scale it. How to accelerate it, change it, or keep it as a lifestyle business.

Looking at businesses this way allows the company to *tell you* what the growth strategy is. This is critically important to the entire process of finding your match.

In Eric Reis' *The Lean Startup*, he coined the term *pivot* to describe changes during entrepreneurial product development. Always turning to user data and customer feedback to tweak the next iteration of the product in order to build the product the market wants and attain product-market fit.

In management, this happens all the time—it just doesn't look like a startup. Companies need to innovate. Perhaps not constantly, but at very specific times. Staying plugged in to an industry's changing demands is what keeps companies going long term.

When you look at a company, try to find what it brings to the table. Look for the opportunity in the company and in the industry. Identify how good the company is at being able to execute on the opportunity—what it has and what it lacks. If your strengths and goals are a good fit for executing the growth opportunity, potentially unlocking its hidden value, you've just found your platform.

This makes the search a bit more of a dance. You first identify your strengths, then match it to the growth opportunity the potential acquisition offers. When the match is right, you stop looking and move forward.

Defining the type of growth opportunity you seek in a target acquisition is very different from how most people approach the business-buying process, and perhaps the reason why so many fail to buy once they start looking—they don't know what they're looking for in the first place. After buying half a dozen companies and looking at ten times that many, no broker has ever asked me what type of growth opportunity I'm looking for. Instead, they want to know what industries I've worked in and try to apply that to targets. You can see how this structure doesn't move the buyer forward with confidence when they start looking at potential companies.

Now, I want you to clearly define the growth opportunity you are looking for. Is it a company that needs to build a sales team? Improved marketing? New distribution channels? Financial engineering? Operational improvement? Or a customer base in a certain market? The truth is, you already know. Identifying this clearly is the first part of what will become your target statement.

SIZE

When it comes to buying a company, size matters. Typically, the size of the target is identified by revenue but then valued on a multiple of SDE or cash flow. Now that you know which type of company profile you want to purchase, you'll need to identify the target SDE.

As a result, defining what you are looking for by revenue is just the wrong metric. What if you find a software-as-a-service company with 70 percent net income to revenue? Or a metal-trading company with 1 percent net income? Defining by revenue doesn't define your target by the thing you are buying in the first place: the cash flow.

Instead, define the target by the amount of SDE. To review, the Seller Discretionary Earnings (SDE), is a measure of how much total cash flow the seller of the firm has been enjoying. It is calculated by taking the pre-tax earnings of a company, then adding back any interest and non-cash expenses like amortization and depreciation (which will give you Earnings Before Interest, Taxes, Depreciation, and Amortization). Finally, adding in any seller benefit such as salary, personal insurance and vehicles, and any one-time expenses the company had during that time.

As listings move from Main Street to middle market, a definition largely defined by size, you'll likely see Adjusted EBITDA as the metric used instead of SDE. They typically refer to the same thing. The difference is often that Adjusted EBITDA is the term largely used for passive ownership, while SDE refers to active ownership.

Despite all the complicated valuation calculations that can be done to calculate value, the typical transaction just comes down to identifying the SDE (or Adjusted EBITDA) number by a fair multiple. The smaller the firm, the smaller the multiple. Typically, you'll see good companies under $700,000 in SDE trading at two and a half to three and a half times SDE, and companies over $700,000 at north of that. Companies that have $2,000,000 in Adjusted EBITDA will get the attention of private equity firms and will drive multiples up due to competition of these professional buyers. Private equity activity has been dropping to lower levels in recent years due to the large cash reserves and increasing quantity of companies below $2,000,000.

As a result, I have found that the most "affordable" acquisitions for financial buyers and acquisition entrepreneurs can be had in the $250,000 to $700,000 SDE range. The multiples remain lower, at two and a half to three and a half, but can push toward four if the revenue and earnings have experienced strong growth.

By no means am I suggesting you focus on this same segment. The more capital you have access to and the larger the company is equates to increased stability in an organization. If you are in a position to acquire a more solidly middle-market firm, you should explore that option.

In addition, many acquisition entrepreneurs starting out might not go it alone. They can bring in partners with capital to invest or apply for backing by the many search funds that are supporting these entrepreneurs with training, search efforts, and financial backing. The size you are looking for can change quickly with the involvement of partners or investors.

Firms with north of $1 million in Adjusted EBITDA can provide a cushion in cash flow, the managing of which will quickly top your list of priorities after closing. It allows for higher salaries, more dollars to reinvest, or hiring of additional management when you need it, for example. These companies will typically be $5 to $20 million in revenue and, statistically, will provide a significant increase in security to the buyer.

A side note on multiples: you might be of the opinion that the multiples I suggested above (two and a half to four) are low. They would be in certain segments or to certain buyers. A strategic buyer would be another company already in the space and with existing infrastructure that could benefit more from the acquisition than an acquisition entrepreneur, who would be considered a "financial buyer" in this case. The strategic buyer would be willing to pay more for the company and could push multiples up. That said, in the example above, we are talking about a very specific SDE range, and support for this argument has repeated many years in a row by Pepperdine Private Capital Market Reports.[40]

By measuring an acquisition target by SDE instead of revenue, you are defining the search by the cash flow it will provide and the transaction price you can afford, so it will become part of your target statement.

You can find a simple acquisition modeling tool to help you define your target by size at *BuyThenBuild.com*. This will help calculate the amount of equity you would need to close on a certain-sized business. Or, if you prefer, help identify what size business you can acquire with the amount of cash you have to invest. But let's walk through how the calculation works here.

An overly simple way to calculate what you can afford based on the available cash you have to invest looks like this (be warned, this is very loose math and should be used only to give you an approximate value range of what you can currently afford and the different ways the variables can impact the outcome):

Let's say X is the amount of liquid capital you have available to put toward buying a company.

Take X and divide by 10 percent to get the purchase price (PP) of the business at a 90 percent leveraged position. This is the minimum amount of capital that can be injected via a bank loan and does assume minimum asset values in the company. Only

---

40   https://bschool.pepperdine.edu/institutes-centers-research/centers/applied-research/
     content/private-capital-markets-report-2017.pdf

injecting 10 percent of the purchase price will increase your risk but maximize your ROI.

$$X / 0.1 = PP$$

The purchase price, as we have covered, is derived by paying a multiple (M) of Seller Discretionary Earnings (SDE).

$$PP = SDE \times M$$

Dividing both sides by M reverses the equation to determine what the SDE would be, given a specific purchase price and multiple.

$$PP / M = SDE$$

This will help you determine what SDE range you can currently afford, given the amount of debt you can manage, or how much capital you need to raise prior to going to the bank to fund the rest.

Other considerations will include Accounts Receivable minus Accounts Payable and Inventory, as well as any additional working capital you might choose to add. Closing costs at the bank are also allowed to be rolled into the loan, so you'll have to pay 10 percent of those fees up front. In addition, and especially at high debt levels, you'll want to keep cash aside should the company get tight on cash.

Let's run through a hypothetical example.

Nancy has decided she'd like to buy a company. She's managed to save $200,000 over her career outside of retirement accounts, which she's decided to use toward business acquisition purposes.

She knows she'll need a little for working capital and closing costs.

Working capital will include AR – AP + Inventory, as well as any additional cash she wants in the company on day one.

She estimates $100,000 in AR – AP, $100,000 in inventory, and $100,000 in additional cash at closing.

According to SBA.gov, fees associated with a $5,000,000 loan are $138,125.[41] She doesn't plan on taking a loan quite that high, so she assumes there will be $100,000 in SBA and bank fees. This equates to $400,000 she'll need for total working capital and closing. Ninety percent of which can be borrowed from the bank, so she sets aside 10 percent of her own cash in that amount, or $40,000.

She then decides that she wants some reserves and decides she'll hold back $60,000, leaving $100,000 to acquire a company.

$$\$200,000 \text{ available} – \$40,000 – \$60,000 = \$100,000$$
$$\text{for investment}$$

She takes $100,000 and divides it by 10 percent to give her the purchase price.

$$\$100,000 / 0.1 = \$1,000,000$$

She takes her purchase price of $1,000,000 and decides that she wants a company that is a little stronger than average. Something that isn't a turnaround and the seller could reasonable defend a multiple over the average of three for companies of that size. She decides 3.2 is a good estimate.

$$\$1,000,000 / 3.2 = \$312,500$$

---

41 For a $5,000,000 loan (75 percent of which is guaranteed to the lending bank, or $3,750,000), the loan fee is $138,125 calculated as 3.5 percent of the first $1 million guaranteed ($35,000) plus 3.75 percent of the remaining guaranteed amount.

This gives her an annual SDE amount of $312,500. From there, Nancy knows that SDE amounts typically range from 10 to 20 percent of revenue, so unless she's looking at a highly profitable or a low profit company, the revenue of the target should fall in the $1.5 million to $3.1 million range ($312,500 / 0.1 and $312,500 / 0.2). She then calculates the debt service payments assuming a 6 percent interest rate over ten years and subtracts it from the SDE. This comes out to $165,853 in pre-tax cash flow after debt service.

Nancy concludes for a $140,000 total investment, she is able to generate $165,853 pre-tax, or 118 percent, in annual return to balance between personal income and reinvestment in the company.

After working with the numbers, Nancy decides that she is comfortable describing her target company as having an SDE of $300,000 to $350,000 and will apply this knowledge when putting together her target statement.

She calculates that if she is able to grow the company 10 percent every year, it will exceed $4 million in revenue, the debt will be paid off, and she could be making over $700,000 a year. She begins to see buying a business as a vehicle for driving creativity, utilizing her strengths, and building wealth.

Armed with the opportunity profile you are looking for, as well as a defined SDE range for that target, you're well on your way to having your target statement put together. Finally, you need to define the core industry type.

INDUSTRY TYPE

Which specific industry you decide to acquire in is important, but during a search you should not limit yourself by looking at one specific industry. As you've hopefully seen in the prep work you have done, industry is not the driver for many people's success.

Instead, defining the industry by general type, such as manufacturing, distribution, product, online, or service allows for defining
the target company with the right metric, but also the ability to throw
your search net further, resulting in more opportunities for review.

I believe that industries all have similar characteristics and are
more alike than different, so by identifying the target business by
type is the better way to approach the search.

That said, many really do have true valuable relationships in
certain industries. If you've worked for a decade in a specific industry and have true relationships with buyers, then it will likely be
faster for you to get traction in that industry. Still, look really hard
at those relationships before you take them for granted. Most buyers
of any product or service will actually stay with the company rather
than switch when their sales person or representative moves to
a competitor.

In the same regard, you may have some industry-specific knowledge. Although it might benefit you in the short term, if you acquire
a company in a different industry, but with requiring similar skillsets,
you are able to transfer your experience and apply it in a new arena.
This typically adds to greater insights and perhaps new, better ways
of doing things.

Many venture capital firms like to see entrepreneurs with past
success—but not in the industry they're going into. You've seen some
of this in corporate training programs as well, where no related
experience is actually better because the new recruits don't bring
"bad habits" with them.

The point here is simply to share that if you have business
experience in a specific industry, look very closely at it. Are these
experiences truly going to bring value, like customer relationships,
or are they your own desire to stay out of the learning curve of a

new industry? If the latter, I encourage you to look at what you bring to the table and expand your search by defining the target by type instead of something specific.

Sometimes defining what you are looking for by a specific industry is exactly the right thing to do. If you're a dentist, then it should be clear what type of business you're going to buy. The same could go for a lawyer, accountant, or financial advisor. Often, these are easy to launch as a side business, but acquiring a practice from a retiring small firm or even having a rollup strategy around service firms can be a great strategy.

CPA John Bly, author of *Cracking the Code: An Entrepreneurs' Guide to Growing Your Business Through Mergers and Acquisitions for Pennies on the Dollar*, has done just this with his accounting firm, LBA Haynes Strand, PLLC. John has shown incredible growth with his firm by growing through acquisition. Buying a company to get started is a completely viable strategy. Defining industry specifically is often critical when considering growing your existing business through acquisition, but not with a platform company.

More likely than not, defining your target industry by type will provide more opportunities to review that still fit your objective. So I encourage you to go as wide as possible with your definition of industry.

PRODUCT, DISTRIBUTOR, SERVICE

All business can probably be identified as offering a product, acting as a distributor, or providing a service. These are the main industry types you should use to structure your target statement. The choice of which one best fits you might be obvious already.

If you are looking for a product, are you wanting to be a manufacturer or simply a reseller of that product? A product company could be a manufacturing company, or one that simply owns the right to the brand, manufactures the product from a supplier, and manages the sales channels.

One example of how this might play out is that many manufacturers have been around for a long time, are product forced, and have legacy systems in place, including in their marketing. If you thrive on the idea of introducing digital marketing to a product you can get behind, perhaps this is an area for you to consider. In other words, you might be wanting to find a manufacturing company, not because of the manufacturing, but because of the growth opportunity provided by a lack of online marketing. The industry type could be "backed into" by a specific growth opportunity. This is why looser definitions on industry are better at the early stages.

Distribution companies can source, manage inventory, coordinate international logistics, or be a reseller of a product. A core competency in distribution could be applied to logistics management, channel management, supply chain efficiencies, or product reselling.

The service industry employs more than 33 percent of the world's labor force. It includes all professional services like legal and accounting, banking, advertising, software engineering, IT, medicine, nonprofit activity, education, and retail or custom light-manufacturing.

These three industry types of product, distribution, or service stand as three different offerings, or values, to the market, and are probably the biggest three differentiators among deciding on an industry. Make a decision to anchor your statement in one or two of these industry types in order to bring a little focus to a broad description. We want your description to be specific enough that people understand what you are looking for, but not so specific that the opportunity never turns up. Getting the balance right may require further reflection on your part to identify the specific industry drivers you prefer.

Once you have decided the industry type, consider referring to the *Business Brokerage Press' Business Reference Guide*.[42] This is a wonderful reference for determining trends, valuations, margins, expense breakdowns, other benchmark data, and expert comments. Once you start working with brokers, they will all have a copy they can reference for you, but at just over twenty dollars per month for an online subscription, I find it's a great way to explore all the possibilities before getting lost in the details of specific deals. It will also help you later, while previewing potential opportunities, to know whether you are looking at a standard, sub-standard, or optimal performance for the industry in which it's in. It's a minor cost for such a transparent view.

LIMITERS

The final step prior to forming your target statement is to apply a bit of the process of elimination. We need to identify any limiters that apply to your search, anything that you absolutely don't want to consider. This will bring focus to your activity by filtering out anything not worth considering.

The top limiter is geographic preferences. Are you okay moving wherever the best opportunity is? Or do you require staying in the same location? If you need to work around where you are, how far are you willing to commute? Or, are you looking for an online business where the company is often completely relocatable?

Are there any industries you absolutely will not work in? How would you define those in the most general way? What if purchasing

---

42 *http://businessreferenceguide.com*

real estate isn't available? What if it is required? Take some time to reflect and decide how you think about these things so that you are prepared when they get introduced later.

TARGET STATEMENT

In this chapter you've applied your skillset to identify the type of opportunity you're looking for, worked through the size of the company you'd like to target, and defined your industry type and applied any limiters.

One of the reasons only 10 percent of potential buyers ever succeed in acquiring a company is that they go months or years without identifying what you've put together in this chapter alone. They kick tires and waste time, never realizing the shortcomings of their actions.

Now it's time to pull all of this together in your *target statement*. This is what you will use as your compass as you start your search journey. It goes like this:

> **I am looking for a** *[choose product, distribution, or service]* **company with** *[enter the type of growth opportunity]*, **generating** *[define size by SDE range]*, **with** *[enter any limiters]*.

The order isn't critical and you can eliminate any part that doesn't apply to you, but it's important that all aspects are considered. Here are a few examples:

> "I am looking for a distribution company with strong sales and marketing processes but needing operational excellence, generating $300,000 to $400,000 in Seller Discretionary Earnings, in or around the Chicago area."

"I am looking for a manufacturing company with no current eCommerce presence, generating $250,000 to $300,000 in SDE."

"I'm looking for a commercial IT service business with solid operations but lacking a strong B2B sales effort, generating between $750,000 and $1,000,000 in SDE in the regional southwest."

"I am looking for any service company tied to real estate with a direct sales effort needed as the driver for growth, generating between $400,000 and $500,000, located in the greater Portland area."

Spend time and get your statement right. It's the first piece of the most common question regarding acquisition entrepreneurship, which we'll address in the next chapter.

CHAPTER 5

THE SEARCH

INEVITABLY, AFTER INTRODUCING THE CONCEPT OF ACQUISI-tion entrepreneurship, the first question I get is, "Yes, *but how do you find these companies?*" This chapter answers that question.

Many start a business acquisition search by hitting some of the listing sites online and seeing what's for sale. The serious buyers begin reaching out to brokers or intermediaries after that. Out of the few potential buyers that get a true search going, only about one out of ten eventually buy a business. Obviously, the current process is flawed or there would be greater success rates.

But the high level of confidentiality, inexperienced buyers and sellers, and the fragmented nature of listing and transacting businesses has created a lot of opacity around navigating the landscape. In short, there are three things most people do that you need to ignore: skip the internet, don't commit to one broker, and don't depend only on listings. These are all tools that can be used, but you need to define the process for yourself. The business you are looking for is out there, and your first job as CEO is to go find it.

In the previous chapters we've been prepping you for success. If you skipped them and came right to this chapter on the search, I don't blame you since it's the first thing everyone wants to know, but building the proper mindset, exploring the Three As, and defining your target statement are all prerequisites to starting a successful search in the first place. Skipping them puts you right back in the broken process with everyone else.

SKIP THE INTERNET

Most people start by finding a popular site like *bizbuysell.com* and spending an inordinate amount of time, often during leisure time, passively reviewing the listings. Whatever you do, do not do this. You do need to get familiar with sites like this and what's on them, but plugging into this habit as your end game will stifle your effort from the start.

First, do not go to these sites during leisure time. This isn't shopping for a t-shirt you like and simply passing over the ones that don't look good. This is potentially the most serious search you've ever performed, and you will *not* do it passively.

Having the right mindset during the search includes your absolute commitment to finding the right business and buying it within six months. This is completely possible for serious buyer, and it's completely possible for prepared buyers who have gone through the first chapters of this book.

Having this commitment is critical. You need to understand that getting financing or pulling investors together will take time. Due diligence takes time. The legal back and forth takes time. Things can go wrong, and you might have to walk away from a bad deal, extend due diligence, or perhaps have the seller back out. All of these can delay your outcome. Being aware of these possibilities will have you organized and working with a sense of urgency that most buyers simply lack. You are not a tire kicker; you are clear, motivated, goal-oriented, and prepared.

So, get organized like this is your job, because it is. Set a folder aside for listings, start a spreadsheet as you look at listings and record industry, location, revenue, asking price, and any other critical or comparative information you can use later.

I do want you to go online and look at listings because you'll get familiar with what's out there, the different ways to search and review, and you can get additional information without wasting too much of an advisor's time. It's a great practice ground. It will also help you identify what's publicly listed later when a broker hands you a stack of easily sourced listings—you'll be able to know what came from them and what's already out there. You can find a list of these sites on *BuyThenBuild.com*.

But here's the deal: your company is very likely not on this website.

There are three possible types of businesses on these sites: junk, non-growth, or good. By "non-growth," I'm referring to laundromats, car washes, and restaurants. Go ahead and consider these as investments if it suits you, but the growth-minded acquisition entrepreneur is either looking for a company that is scalable, or developing a strategy around how to leverage the fact that they're all available. Regardless of which type it is, they will also be on the smaller end, so the larger amount of SDE or Adjusted EBITDA[43] you're looking for, the less likely you'll find it there.

The point is that although there are good listings on these online marketplaces, it's hard to find them mixed in with all the other stuff. Further, they will be the first to sell, making the other two categories more readily available. By surveying over time, you'll be able to see what gets sold and what stays.

---

43   Seller Discretionary Earnings (SDE) or commonly referred to as cash flow.

In addition, brokers will increase the amount of potential buyers by putting it online, which makes more work for them as they need to filter through potentially "bad" buyers. This is an inefficiency they need to manage, so they'll typically put it on an online marketplace only after they've reached out to vetted buyers and their professional network. Which brings us to the lesson: *you need to get upstream.*

In investment banking and private equity, professionals look for "deal flow." Since they are evergreen professional buyers, what typically differentiates the pros in the business is "who has the deal." Getting the best deal flow means that a firm is always at the top of the list for potential sellers and somehow gets early looks at the best opportunities. The opacity and fragmentation of the market allows for this and makes navigating deal flow a major part of what makes a good firm—they get access to the good deals!

This is exactly what you are trying to achieve, and I assure you professional buyers aren't hanging out exclusively on bizbuysell. Instead, you need to get out and meet the people who have deal flow in your area. In your case, this is the business brokers, intermediaries, I-bankers, and M&A Advisors[44] who get the listings in the first place.

If you need proof of this, I would ask you to draw on your own experience looking for a job online. Using online job post sites like Monster and CareerBuilder can work, but more than likely, focusing on them just kills your job search. This is because they are mostly geared toward entry-level candidates who aren't networked well,

---

44 To revisit, all of these are different words for essentially the same thing. Often, the term is defined by the transaction size that a firm targets, but in every case it is the individual who has the business listed to sell or who helps buyers find potential acquisition targets. In most cases, outside Main Street business brokers, they can also help arrange for capital, thus the term "investment banker."

they are postings that generate thousands of applicants, and frankly, if the company couldn't find anyone they knew to hire for the job, then it ends up on a website as an afterthought. All the jobs aren't bad, but most of them are, and the great jobs never find themselves on an online job posting site. Finding a job that is a good fit for your skillset is probably 90 percent networking. Finding a business is no different.

This trend exists at every level of the market, from Main Street to solidly middle-market investment bankers, from bizbuysell to Axial.net; the deal doesn't hit the website if they can engage a buyer before they have to. These sites exist for people who do not have deal flow themselves. Yet at least 80 percent of the private equity professionals I know that pay the high fees to services like Axial have expressed in one way or another that they aren't there to get the *specific* deals on the platform. Instead, they are there to learn *who has the deals*, then build relationships with them. They're using the marketplaces to get upstream, not for the specific listings. It's time to take a page out of their book and get hustling.

Before moving on from website listings, however, I want to share a clear exception. In my experience, business brokerage firms who exclusively sell online businesses only tend to have a very well-executed online listing strategy. I believe this to be for three core reasons.

First, they are a specific firm showing their specific listings, as opposed to a posting site where all sites can come to post various businesses. They are not posting to the world, but through their community of mostly vetted buyers. In addition, because online companies tend to have close to no employees and zero customer concentration, concerns around confidentiality are significantly reduced. There is no risk of destroying morale or throwing a key customer account into question. As a result, these listings are inherently more upstream than online marketplaces.

Second, online companies typically eliminate the number one most common limiter for a buyer's search—geographic restrictions really don't apply. This means that for buyers who have already defined their skillset and desired opportunity, finding listings in this specific niche can be pretty streamlined online.

Third, and perhaps the most important, online-based companies are extremely transferrable. Because their assets are all virtual and typically operate with just one or two people, an entire business can be transferred in just a couple of hours. Further, the amount of quantifiable data direct from known third party entities like Google, Amazon, and eBay can make it very simple to validate all the information associated with a business like this.

As a result, there are some very good business brokerage sites with very good, vetted listings. That said, this does not mean their good listings are reason to skip direct communication with the brokers.

As a case in point, one eCommerce business I bought myself came from direct outreach from the founder of one such online brokerage firm. He was reaching out to a dozen people who had seriously looked at other businesses very similar in nature and size. Since I already knew what I was looking for via my target statement, I was able to move fast, secure a Letter of Intent within a couple business days of hearing about the opportunity, and eventually acquire the largest dedicated online distributor of upflush toilets and macerating water pumps.

Getting past the internet listings and getting upstream to the brokers themselves will help generate your own deal flow. Anything that ends up on the online marketplaces has already been shown to those buyers known to the listing broker, as well as likely other brokers in the same or neighboring firms. Once no one they know buys it, it can get listed on the internet (perhaps their own site first, then the marketplaces later).

BROKER OUTREACH

In 1951, the famous criminal "Slick Willie" Sutton[45] reportedly answered the question, "Why do you rob banks?" with, "Because that's where the money is." The analogy is not that buying businesses is like robbing banks, but rather that going to the source of what you want is the fastest and most direct method. Indeed, sussing out brokers who manage businesses for sale for a living is the fastest and most direct way to get to the company you will acquire.

Fragmented markets, like the buying and selling of companies, typically results in enormous variances in quality. This industry is no different. Brokers and intermediaries unfortunately have to deal with large variances in potential buyers. The buyer with the most variance will be the first-time buyer. If you're reading this, this likely describes you—someone who has never bought a company before.

The reasons are obvious: some don't know what they are looking for, some don't have the money, some don't have the right mindset or commitment, so even if they do eventually find a company they should acquire, they won't be able to pull the trigger. Since brokers are paid when deals close and their reputation will be made by the number of closed deals. Most are reluctant to take on first-time buyers given this trait.

---

45   Robert M. Yoder, "Someday They'll Get Slick Willie Sutton," *The Saturday Evening Post* 223:30, p.17, January 20, 1951.

This is exactly why the first time I tried to buy a company in 2004, my initial search ended in failure. I had no way to navigate the industry, brokers didn't take me seriously, and the companies that were for sale that I was able to see were bottom-of-the-barrel listings. I certainly didn't have the insight to develop a target statement. This will not be you! You have the mindset, the commitment, the preparation to know what you are looking for and to motivate the brokers to work for you.

Most potential buyers who get past the internet listings and do reach out to a broker will usually find a broker and then just use that broker over time. Let's take a lesson from notorious economists Steven Levitt and Stephen Dubner's book,[46] *Freakonomics,* and identify how brokers are incentivized.

How intermediaries are compensated varies a little. A Main Street broker and a Wall Street investment banker have different services they offer, but in either case they will make 90–100 percent of their compensation *when a transaction occurs.*

To get a transaction to occur, they need a capable buyer and willing seller to come to an agreement on price. At the end of the day, that's it.

I'm not going to say that brokers are heartless, selfish people, but understanding the economics will highlight a couple key components. For example, they don't really care about the exact sale price of a company. They might make anywhere from 2–8 percent on a million this direction or that. That's not nothing, but not closing a deal is nothing—they get nothing. So, they'd rather transact a deal at the wrong price than not at all.

---

46 As an aside, Levitt and Dubner's fourth book, *When to Rob a Bank...* could have taught Slick Willie Sutton a lesson. The economic answer is "never," because the Return on Investment is terrible.

If you are a new broker, the first thing you set out to do is to go out and get listings.[47] If you have listings, then some percentage of them will transact, even if you don't have a rolodex of buyers yourself yet. The broker simply needs to circulate their listings to other brokers and potential buyers. The listing will get circulated to the other intermediaries at the firm and other firms to see if they can generate immediate interest. Typically, this takes the form of an email blast to their private, vetted email signups.

If there is no interest in this preliminary outreach within network, it ends up on some version of the internet. This is how both intermediaries new to the industry as well as industry seniors do it. The only difference is that the seniors have built a career and usually an expansive network over time, so typically the businesses considering selling come to them.

Wouldn't you like to be upstream and get first look at the companies considering selling? This is a hypothetical question, of course, since this is where the majority of the quality opportunities lie. As a result, you'll need to create a plan to reach out to all in your area who can help you and begin building a network.

In order to get upstream, you'll need to get your house in order first. Put together your personal balance sheet (resources available to help you on *BuyThenBuild.com*), network with any potential equity backers if needed,[48] and search the internet for business brokers, business intermediaries, and investment bankers in your

---

47 Listings, of course, are businesses listed for sale.

48 An equity backer is not a lending institution like a bank who will offer debt for the acquisition, but rather a parent, friend, partner, angel investor, or investment group. Often, potential buyers in a search claim they have a "backer," meaning if they are not in a position to inject all the required capital investment, they have a passive investor who is interested in backing them. Some top business schools have begun to invest in small business acquisition for their alumni.

city. Look on LinkedIn. Make a list of these as you go along with contact information for each one. You are going to try to meet with all of them.

As we highlighted, this is where many fall short. First-time buyers will reach out to one and start working with that person. This makes sense given that it's similar to buying a home, where we may hire a buyer's agent to take us around to all kinds of homes. This works in real estate, but I believe one of the main reasons many buyers don't execute once they start a search is because they begin to rely on one person in a greatly fragmented market.

Remember that brokers get listings? Well, you're going to do an outreach directly to those who have the listings. You do not require Joe for you to have a conversation with Jill to discuss her listings.

In conclusion, Phase 1 of your search is to meet with every intermediary in your area, explain what you're looking for, review their current listings, and get on their email list for new listings. This will result in you getting vetted and upstream to the deal flow in your area.

Time to start calling or emailing to request those meetings.

MEETING BROKERS

During your first meeting with an intermediary, they want to know three things:

First, and at the very basic level, how do you present your-self? Are you someone they could introduce to potential sellers with confidence?

Second, do you have the money? Are you capable of pulling the trigger on an acquisition if they find one?

Third, what type of business are you looking for?

The first point is obvious. Be on time. Dress intelligently. Let them know that you've been reading books on the process to "get smart" about buying a business and analyzing what you are looking for. Follow up with a "thank you" email after the meeting, highlighting next steps. Just do the basic things that professionals do. If you have a personal balance sheet available and your resume ready to email after the meeting, you will thrill them with your preparedness and professionalism. Explain that you understand that most searches fail. Most buyers they spend their time with are a waste. Let them know that you are committed to buying a company within six months. Remember, you're trying to recruit their help and you need to fill them with confidence that you are worth them spending time on. The conviction of a timeline is something they rarely see—especially on a first meeting.

Second, do you have the money? If brokers could, they would ask this before they ask your name. To get a deal closed will take a lot of time and effort on their part. It's committed work for six to eighteen months, depending on how it goes. Making sure they have a buyer who isn't going to leave them at the altar is critical.

Brokers need to figure this out on the first meeting because if you don't have the capital to pull the trigger on a business, then they will be wasting months of their time. This is what I mean when I say, "capable buyer." *Does the buyer have the means to transact?* This is the question they will need answered immediately.

If you have enough money to buy a company in all cash, great—this is easy. If you don't, it's critical that you have an equity "backer" set up before you begin your outreach to brokers. If you don't, you will destroy your first impression with the key people you will need to help you execute. If brokers smell a smoke screen or that you're going to put it on them to negotiate seller financing, you're out.

I received an email last week from an acquisition entrepreneur who had gotten a company under Letter of Intent to purchase. He was raising 30 percent of the purchase price from investors via an email outreach campaign. This was keeping him from having to put any of his own money into buying the company. This is an advanced tactic and one that a first-time buyer won't be able to get past the broker unless you have relationships with intermediaries savvy in middle-market financial engineering. My guess is that the buyer had the capital themselves or else they would not get that far in the process. So, it is possible, but this is not the book on how to buy a company with no money down.

Brokers want to feel good that you have the means, and they'd like to know that you have at least 50 percent of the purchase amount in accessible, liquid assets. If you have your personal balance sheet that shows this, take it with you for discussion. You don't need to leave it behind, but be ready to review it with them. Discuss how you are aware that banks lend on business acquisitions based on the hard assets, and that you are capable of getting a loan. If you get brokers comfortable that you have the means or the backing, you've just won a partner who will spend time helping you on your journey.

Also, remember that this interview is two-way. Intermediaries have a huge variance in quality and style and you need to determine what type of professional you're talking to. If there is a head broker of the firm, make sure your first meeting is with them. That's who you want to work with because they know the most people, or they will be able to direct you to the right broker in their firm who is best for you.

Does the firm validate any information? Do they review and vet listings? How do they go about getting listings? Do they specialize in certain industries? Who else do they know that can help you on your search? Does the broker have business management experience?

Were they an owner at one point themselves? How did they come to becoming an intermediary? Are they a licensed broker? How are they compensated? These are all questions you will want to know.

A couple notes on this: whether a broker is FINRA licensed[49] or not has not mattered in my experience practicing acquisition entrepreneurship. In almost all cases in the lower middle market, the buyer prefers an asset purchase versus a stock purchase. There also seems to be a reverse correlation between whether a broker is licensed and whether they have ever owned their own company. Typically, FINRA licensed brokers tend to have had longer careers in the services industry. They might have been a stock broker, banker, CPA, or financial planner prior, rather than a business owner or entrepreneur. That said, licensed brokers who have had careers in the financial services industry will typically transact bigger companies than those that don't.

There are a few certifications that are meaningful when evaluating a broker which you can be on the lookout for. First is the obvious MBA or other business degree. Then there are a number of programs that stress best practices in the industry. For example, the Certified M&A Advisor (CMAA) offered by the Alliance of M&A Advisors (AMAA); the Certified Business Intermediary (CBI) by the International Business Brokers Association (IBBA); the M&A Master Intermediary (M&AMI) by the M&A Source, and the Certification in Private Capital Markets at Pepperdine University's

---

49 The Financial Industry Regulatory Authority (FINRA) is the organization that oversees regulation, enforcement, and arbitration around selling stock, such as the New York Stock Exchange, broker dealers, and exchange markets. They are a division of the US Government's Securities and Exchange Commission (SEC). When I was a stock broker during the tech bust, I was licensed with a Series 7 and 63 through FINRA so that I could buy and sell stock. Many brokers are not licensed because it's not required for asset sales, nor for providing their main service of bringing buyers and sellers together and navigating the transaction.

Graziadio Business School are all reputable programs in the industry, bringing professionalism, research, and best practices to the industry. Brokers who participate with these organizations tend to have higher levels of professionalism and stronger networks, which can provide increased deal flow.

In my experience, a broker who is a former business owner or entrepreneur brings incredible value to a deal simply because they understand more intimately the intangibles and the emotional aspects that the buyer and seller will go through.

Brokers who screen their listings are taking on a different level of responsibility than those who don't. This does not mean you don't want to work with those who don't, but you need to be aware that everything you look at from the beginning should be assumed to be false, since the broker takes no responsibility to qualify their listings. This will make due diligence longer and even more critical.

After the broker gets comfortable with you and your ability to transact, they'll ask you the third question: *what type of business you're looking for.*

This is the exact question that misleads many buyers. Those who haven't spent the time going through the funnel examining attitude and aptitude, and defining action, opportunity, and size will start a search that never ends. They'll suggest an industry, and the broker will go to work to find something close. This results in loosely defined targets and tire kicking. This will not be you. This is when you explain to them that you define what you are looking for not in revenue but in SDE, not in industry but in opportunity, and you hit them with your prepared *target statement* we defined in the last chapter.

Before the end of the meeting, negotiate a glimpse into their current listings. Don't ask for more information on all of them, just review them together and go deeper on no more than two or three if they look like they might match your criteria. Build confidence with your new teammate; be selective and don't spin their wheels.

Before departing, ask them to keep your target statement in mind as they come across potential sellers over the following months. Ask if you can set up another meeting in a month to touch base, and get on their mailing list.

Many intermediaries will want to help you without any commitment at this point. Some may try to engage you in a buyer's agent contract where you pay them a monthly fee for an outbound search. You do not have to do this. I've met with intermediaries who don't have active listings and they are typically the ones wanting to engage in a paid search.

My perspective is that it's the brokers who have the listings and the deal flow. As long as you are out there talking with all of them, you'll know where the deals are. Moreover, once you meet with half a dozen, you'll know who you can count on to help you find the company you're looking for.

EVERY BUSINESS IS FOR SALE

Where do intermediaries find listings? Listings are current businesses where, after talking to a broker who reached out to them, the owner has expressed an interest in potentially selling.

I like listings a lot because the broker has spent time with the seller, prepped them on the valuation of their company, and spent time getting the seller to the point where they are willing to explore a sale. Also, as you get into the acquisition process, you'll experience first-hand the tremendous benefit having a broker in the deal provides.

Often, sellers go through a process of their own to get to a point where they are ready to sell. Typically, all owners think their business is worth significantly more than the going valuations. Once they get their arms around this fact, it takes them a while to decide to sell rather than keep the business. This is because if they're only going to get two and a half to five times the annual SDE, they may be tempted to keep it, thinking they can get the same amount of money over the next three years.

It's also their baby! Countless hours working to build the company, and developing working relationships with their employees and customers means they have grown roots with this lifestyle. It's a big decision.

That said, brokers reach out to business owners every day seeing if they would like to sell their company, and some agree to explore it. The truth is that every business is for sale, and you can do the bird-dogging just as they can.

The third time I tried to acquire a company, I tried to do it without a broker at all. This was around 2011, and I was wanting to grow my company's infrastructure through acquisition.

I developed my target statement and then researched companies that might fit the infrastructure I was looking for. After starting conversations with the owners and getting pretty far down the path, I realized the true value of a broker.

You need someone to walk through the valuation with them, to get them ready emotionally, and to negotiate on behalf of what's best for "the deal," and not just the buyer. The seller has a lot to think about, and they might not understand all of those points immediately. It's best to establish an intermediary right away in those discussions.

I often reach out directly to companies I'd like to acquire. Everything from eCommerce and fulfillment to solar engineering. From award winning software startups to 100-plus-year-old factories— they are all at different stages of management, and at some point they will be for sale. The owners are not as far along in the selling process as those who have listed with a broker, but setting up repeat meetings with the owner of a company you'd like to acquire will get you through the process. The odds of it ending without an acquisition are much higher, but any company you would want to buy should receive communication from you or your team.

Think about what company you know of that you would like to run. Although you know absolutely nothing about the company, the first thing is simply knowing that it's attractive to you. I asked myself this question one day, emailed the owner (who happened to be a friend of a friend), and he was in my office within hours. His company wasn't listed for sale, but personal circumstances had him already considering selling. I got to him before an intermediary.

I didn't end up acquiring that company, but I've done this same outreach many times over with great results. Every single prospect I've reached out to was willing to talk about it.

My strategy is typically to reach out directly and start a conversation. If they want to explore, I simply tell them that there is a broker I'm working with who can work confidentially with them on putting together a valuation. If the potential seller likes the valuation, the broker can present it to me and we can go from there. This is a great strategy for getting the ball rolling. If there is a personal relationship or network, it works wonders.

Other times, I identify the companies I'm interested in and recruit an intermediary to reach out to the owner, letting them know that they are working with a buyer that specifically researched and put together a list of just a few companies and their name was on it. This allows for the professionalism of a broker, but also, they are putting their reputation on the line saying they have a buyer for their exact company.

Many brokers will do this for you because you are giving them ammo for better outreach for themselves. If you decide you don't want it but they get a listing, then they benefit as well and can try to sell the business to someone else.

Private equity firms are notorious for doing mailings and email campaigns. A friend of mine recently did a search like this and ultimately found and acquired a household insurance company. I receive emails every week from people raising capital for acquisitions or asking if I'd like to consider selling my company. This fragmented market is alive and well. If you know of a company you'd like to acquire, just ask them. Chances are, they're either ready to talk now, or they're ready to talk later. The willing buyer at the table will usually be the path of least resistance for the seller.

CONCLUSION

Knowing what you're looking for is half of the search. Actually, it's more than half. If you know what you're searching for, you can move forward quickly, with clarity, and you will save months of tire kicking and time wasting. You will be able to behave like a professional buyer, knowing when you like something and why. You will be able to see in short order if it is a real yes, a real no, or something that requires next steps to evaluate whether it is a good fit.

This does not mean to be hasty and act with insufficient consideration; rather, it means that you will have more confidence in your search, in talking with brokers and sellers, and in looking at opportunities.

Probably 40 percent of the time I submit a Letter of Intent to acquire a business, I'll be able to do it within a few days of first seeing the Offering Memorandum (OM) and talking with the seller. Another 30 percent within a month. Being able to act this quickly is beneficial to everyone involved. Not only does time kill all deals, but the opposite is true as well. Moving quickly will move you to the frontrunner position as the acquirer, eliminating other potential buyers.

There is a benefit to moving fast, but it's important to move at your own pace. Offer only what is comfortable and only when you are ready. If something is nagging at you, identify what it is and get more information so you can make a clear decision.

In the next chapter, we'll talk about who else you'll need in your network and how to start evaluating the listings.

PART 3

ANALYSIS

"If you change the way you look at things,
the things you look at change."

—WAYNE DWYER

CHAPTER 6

DEAL MAKING

SO FAR, YOU'VE LEARNED THE ECONOMICS OF ACQUIRING A business; you've aligned the Law of Three As, including completing personal assessments around your strengths and weaknesses; you understand the Acquisition Opportunity Profiles Matrix; you've developed your target statement; and you've initiated your search by going upstream.

The amount of preparation you've put into this alone separates you from the vast majority of potential buyers, just so you're aware.

The next step will be bringing a deal together so you can acquire a firm. Managing the web of bank, broker, seller, and maybe even partners is tricky in that you need to sell all of these players on *you* before a specific deal comes to fruition. In this chapter, we'll review the people you'll need on your team, how the initial review of an acquisition target goes, and how all the pieces fit together. These actions should all happen simultaneously on your journey and form the foundation of *deal making*.

Acquiring a company isn't a linear process, and there are some actions you'll need to take now in order to succeed later. There are a lot of moving parts that must be brought together, and none of them exist at the same time. You need to lay the foundation early so that three steps from now you'll be ready and deals don't fall apart because you weren't prepared. Entrepreneurship is the art of creating something out of nothing, creating value where it wasn't before. Bringing a deal together is exactly that. It's the art of making something out of nothing.

For example, investors can't invest without an offer, bankers can't loan without a deal, sellers haven't decided to sell to you (much less at a price that gets a decent return for your investment), brokers can't stop looking for buyers on their listings, and you can't acquire without a company.

The irony of deal making is that you will need to do everything but secure a loan…without a deal on the table.

LEVERAGE

Even if you have enough cash to acquire a company without a loan, you'll still want to take a loan to acquire a business. Why? It's a simple ROI calculation. If you pay $1,500,000 cash for a business and get a 25 percent return, you're happy with your investment. But if you pay $150,000 in a cash-down equity investment, you'll get a 250 percent annual return on the same asset.[50]

Let's back up for a moment and review the amount of leverage that is right for a deal. Please don't conclude that I am suggesting everyone should acquire a company with 90 percent debt. I am only highlighting that it is very possible, given the Small Business Administration (SBA) backs loans at this level. Further, as we saw in Chapter 2, maximizing debt also maximizes the ROI for the investor (i.e. the acquisition entrepreneur, in this case).

That said, you are also maximizing your risk. This is a lesson

---

50   25 percent of $1.5 million is $375,000 in SDE in this example. $375,000 in annual SDE on a $150,000 initial investment is 250 percent annual return.

private equity firms learned in the early 1990s, and now they typically place 30 to 60 percent equity into leveraged buyout (LBO) acquisitions to increase the stability of the investment.[51] Whether you decide to take on this much debt is completely up to you and your banker. Conversely, purchasing a company with all cash will maximize safety but lower the ROI to the absolute minimum. Again, this is up to you. I have known people who have purchased companies at both extremes. The final recipe is up to you (and the bank).

If you are in a position to pay all cash for a specific deal, understand that you're either so wealthy that whatever the deal you'll pay all cash, or you're not thinking big enough. Based on my interviews with brokers, professional buyers, and bankers, very few, if any, high net worth individuals pay all cash for a business. I have to conclude this is because they understand the higher ROI associated with acquiring with some portion on debt—just like PE firms.

Whatever your position, you will likely either desire or require leverage to close on your target company. As a result, you'll need a bank to give you a loan, and I recommend asking for the maximum you can get, for two reasons:

First, you can always take less, and every banker will understand your interest in evaluating a maximum ROI investment. Second, if you don't prep the bank for the maximum you can get at the beginning, then you risk not being able to close on the business a few months down the line. Get access to as much capital as you can and make the decision later.

---

51 That said, the driver of this is somewhat mixed. Private equity firms have an insane amount of liquid capital (currently exceeding $500 billion). If they can't put the capital to use, the investors will pull their money out. In addition, PE firms buy bigger companies that require bigger multiples. So perhaps they put more down to address the additional risk of higher multiples (which you won't have here). So PE firms may be placing larger amounts of capital down to also fill their need to put the money to work. Which is the driver? More stability or more capital working?

Further, if you only invest 10 percent of the purchase price, the payback of that original investment should be returned within the first year; meaning any cash produced after that original return is additional cash flow off that investment...forever.

Here's a quick example: A company is producing an SDE of $400,000 and is acquired at a multiple of 3.2, or $1,280,000. We'll make an assumption here and add $220,000 to cover some working capital, closing costs, lawyer fees, and minor inventory. So, the buyer needs a minimum of $150,000 to inject 10 percent equity investment at closing, with a loan of $1,350,000 to close the deal.

A ten-year, 6 percent[52] interest loan will require $14,987.77 in monthly payments, or about 45 percent of the average monthly cash flow of the business of $33,333.33. This leaves approximately $18,345.56 in average pre-tax monthly cash flow to the acquisition entrepreneur. If all of that went straight to paying back the investor (you), it would take only nine months to pay back the original $150,000 investment. After taxes it will take longer, but this also assumes no growth in the business, which, of course, is a good assumption for calculations, but is not your plan.

Don't have $150,000? Maybe acquisition entrepreneurship isn't for you. However, WWED? Or, What Would an Entrepreneur Do? They would find an investor to sell 10 percent of the company to for $150,000, illustrating that the company is already cash flowing healthily. Plenty of angel investors would take a deal like this. Your job as the CEO of the company you don't have yet is to go find them and get your pitch deck ready.

Sound like a good investment? You'll need a banker.

---

52   SBA rates are typically prime rate + 2.75 percent floating for most banks. Few offer fixed rates, but it is possible.

BANKER OUTREACH

Now that you're actively looking for a business and have started meeting with brokers, you need to start meeting with banks as soon as possible. Not all banks are created equal, and although getting a loan from the right bank will be simple, trying to get a loan from the wrong bank when you have all the pieces in place can kill a deal. So, get started early.

To prepare for meeting with banks, put together your personal balance sheet and pull together your tax returns for the last three years. You can find resources to help you on *BuyThenBuild.com*. In addition, print off a few copies of that resume you put together in Chapter 3. These documents are the cornerstone of what you should bring to the initial meetings.

You'll also want to do a credit check on yourself. Banks are going to need to know whether you qualify as an individual. The assumption of this book is that you, like the business you are going to acquire, are bankable.

Network to find banks that are experienced in business lending and issuing SBA-backed loans. Every community has a list of banks that have issued the most SBA loans. This is a great place to start. Reach out to friends and family and ask for personal introductions to bankers they know. Referrals always play a huge advantage in accelerating trust.

When you interview a bank, start with selling yourself. Present who you are, your experience, and what you are looking to do. Obviously, share with them your target statement as well. Banks work with a lot of small business owners and entrepreneurs and might even know potential sellers. But don't assume they'll share proactively—make sure you ask them specifically. They might be able to put you in touch with someone considering selling.

In the same regard, bankers have exposure to many M&A Advisors. Ask them who they have had exposure to, who they like, and whether they'll help you with an email introduction.

All bankers will try to sell you on why their bank is perfect for you. The driver of the bank business model is in making loans—this is how they make money. However, they also want to be able to turn down deals that don't fit them. Every bank wants to be the first bank to look at a loan opportunity so they can decide whether they want it or not.

Ask them if they do deals like the one you are talking about. Ask them how they feel about real estate loans, small business loans, working capital loans, and whether personal guarantees are required. Ask for examples and referrals. Every referral can also put you in touch with whoever brokered their deal. Are you getting the idea behind this networking thing?

Here's the big secret behind the banks. Whether they are loaning or not is mostly decided by an internal loan-to-deposit (LTD) ratio metric that only the bank knows. Most sustainable business lending banks are going to have somewhere between 60 to 70 percent loan to deposit ratio, while banks in growth mode want to be at a minimum of 90 percent. Bank regulators don't typically get involved unless the banks start getting over 100 percent loan-to-deposit. Finding banks actively looking to give loans is your objective. A hungry bank with a good opportunity (i.e. yours) in hand will be ready to fund quickly.

Loan-to-deposit ratios, however, change with every loan issued. As a result, a bank that's a great fit today might not be in four months. This is why you need to build a network of bankers, because you won't know which is ready when it's time to execute. Of course, don't ask this question outright; it's none of your business. Instead, get a feel for whether it is actively looking for loans and whether you'd be a good fit. The good news is that if it is a bank that is committed to supplying SBA loans, the SBA-backed portion does not affect the bank's ratio, meaning you shouldn't experience a quick change of heart.

I like to get in front of maybe half a dozen bankers at the beginning signs of an opportunity and keep two or three close to me as the deal develops. The other reason for this is having three banks bidding on an opportunity results in the best interest rate at the time of closing. Interest payments on this loan will be a business expense that you are adding to your operational expenses and subtracting from the usable liquid cash flow of your SDE. This means a lower interest rate doesn't just mean a better investment return, but also more cash for salary or reinvestment.

Personally, I favor small local and regional banks, especially those in the middle of executing a growth strategy. They tend to be the most interested in making deals. Building a rapport with the lender is what is going to help make capital available to you. Also, you want to find the right person who understands what you are trying to do and who will really get behind you and support what you're doing. That type of lender will become a part of your team and execute when it comes time to close. A bank can keep your deal from closing, so make sure you court them appropriately, communicating and continually asking them their concerns so you can address them.

Many banks actively looking to grow commonly have a specific SBA lender on staff, which is a signal that the bank has a strategy in alignment with what you are trying to accomplish. Find these people. Specifically, ask them whether they are an SBA preferred lender. If they are, you'll save time in your ability to close, saving over six weeks in some instances. This is because preferred lenders can underwrite the loan in-house rather than working with an external SBA processor.

The SBA's stated mission is to provide capital to small businesses that can't get it on reasonable terms otherwise. The reality is, the SBA is a way banks can make uncollateralized loans. This is because the SBA essentially provides a portion of collateral for the bank. This is why the rates are slightly higher than traditional bank loans. Banks with dedicated SBA lenders on staff and preferred status are clear communication that the bank is looking to grow by supporting acquisition entrepreneurs. They typically hold "PLP" status and can approve SBA loans in house and execute without as much red tape. You want to know these banks and build relationships with them now, before you have a potential deal.

Big national banks, and even large regional banks tend to be mired in red tape and prefer larger clients, so the likelihood of getting a loan, especially as a first-time buyer, is pretty low. Nevertheless, when you're just starting out, you should talk to everyone and learn as much as you can. You never know who you'll meet as a result or what types of opportunities you'll uncover. Bankers will be an important long-term relationship and finding someone you want to work with makes life so much more enjoyable.

Regardless, the bankers will not be able to evaluate your opportunity because you don't have one yet. You don't actually need any money…yet…which is the best time to be meeting and interviewing. Explaining to them that you are mindful of finding a deal where the economics work. I encourage you to engage their assistance in outlining what they are looking for so you can improve your understanding of who the best fit is for what type of deal.

WHAT BANKS LOOK FOR

Ultimately, banks will be looking at the target company's ability to pay back the loan. At the end of the day, that's all they truly require. They look for a minimum debt-to-earnings ratio of 1.25, but often banks will look for more—this is just the minimum. This shouldn't be an issue, because you won't take a potential acquisition to a bank that doesn't have this ratio built in. If the price on the business won't support the debt coverage, it's overpriced and can't afford itself.

Let's take the example from earlier in the chapter with $400,000 in annual SDE and $14,988 in monthly debt service. The annual debt service is $179,853 and the pre-tax cash flow will be $220,147 after the debt is serviced. But non-cash expenses like depreciation will add another $135,000,[53] which will equal earnings of $355,147—or about a 2.0 debt-to-earnings ratio—falling well above the minimum required and giving plenty of room to build a salary for yourself or a reinvestment bucket for business growth.

Many will require some set amount of hard, "bankable" assets—something that can be sold off should the worst-case scenario occur.[54] This situation does make it harder to get an SBA loan for a company that is low asset-intensive, like an internet or software-based company, but typically very easy for even a manufacturing business. In these instances, they'll be looking for a minimum debt-to-earnings ratio of 1.50.

One method used to get around this is to acquire the real estate associated with the business. Typically, a building will add a large amount of bankable assets to a deal and can be purchased through

---

53 $1.35 million in allocated acquisition infrastructure and goodwill over ten years will average to $135,000. This "cost" is depreciated on the income statement but is a non-cash expense.

54 They're managing the downside, just like you.

the same SBA loan you are using to buy the business. An additional benefit is that the addition of real estate into the loan changes the amortization schedule, typically from a ten-year loan to a fifteen- or twenty-five-year loan. This means the per month debt service is lower, allowing a business to build up cash to prepare for a crisis, great opportunity, or to pay down debt. However, you want to really calculate the return on the building investment. Will you outgrow the building? Will you be making business decisions based on real estate holdings? Do you want to be a real estate investor?

Personally, my default is to keep real estate investment opportunities and business opportunities separate. That said, I have acquired buildings in business acquisitions when it becomes a negotiating point later in the deal structure. The benefit is that I am able to build up equity in real estate investments that can be grown over the years ahead. The drawback is that it takes discipline to pay down the business allocated portion of the loan at a faster rate. I prefer to do this because the money in business acquisitions is typically made at the exit, and the more equity buildup you have, the better the cash return to the investor. Keeping the debt associated only with the business will maximize equity buildup for the business.

Other banks will be perfectly comfortable with issuing cash-flow-based loans without hard assets. However, these are typically sizable middle-market-sized deals and not typical of the acquisition entrepreneur until the later stages of success and desire to grow through acquisition.

In situations where the level of hard assets a potential acquisition has is low, the banks will require more cash injection at closing to cover their additional risk. For buyers considering low asset-based acquisitions, Mark Daoust, founder of the exceptional online business specialized brokerage firm, Quiet Light Brokerage, put together an excellent (and often updated) article about buying online businesses with an SBA loan. You can find a link to the article in the resources section at *BuyThenBuild.com*.

ALTERNATIVE DEBT VEHICLES

I've highlighted SBA loans because they have benefits that other debt vehicles or loan types don't share—notably, low equity injection at closing and a government institution backing the loan to the bank itself, which makes the loans easier to acquire. However, SBA loans do have drawbacks.

First, SBA loans are secured. Meaning you'll have to personally guarantee the loan and potentially pledge your house. If the business fails under your watch and it still has a seven-figure principle balance, that's your personal debt to address. This makes the stakes high for the acquisition entrepreneur and likely one of the core reasons such a high percentage of potential buyers don't execute. They never get comfortable with this. Keep in mind you're buying cash flow, supported in part, by bankable assets and a proven track record of product market fit. You're one major step ahead of startups and you get the opportunity to invest in yourself, rather than taking other people's money for ownership in your company. The bank, unlike an investor, doesn't get to participate in your upside success, so although the risks are real, when it all works out this is the best type of investment.

Unsecured commercial loans are possible to get, but it's rare that these loans are offered to a first-time buyer with no track record of managing a company. A bank is going to want the backing of collateral or a government institution like the Small Business Administration every time they can get it. One approach is to acquire the business, get five years of good performance behind you, then renegotiate with the bank. Typically, this will look like a higher interest rate commercial loan, but it's unsecured. You would likely refinance the principle balance of your loan over, say, a seven-year period.

SBA lenders typically will not want the lender to take on a line of credit any time in the first twelve months. However, there is an SBA line of credit called a Cap Line, which plays the role of a line of credit, should there be a need. It's driven almost exclusively on AR and AP aging in the business. Still, you may prefer to over-borrow just to make sure you don't run out of capital due to unforeseen obstacles.

Oddly, SBA-backed loans don't really support seller financing on a deal. Nothing shows support from a seller better than seller financing. However, the SBA dictates that the seller financing has to be over the same term as the SBA loan (ten to twenty-five years), which is significantly longer than traditional seller financing. Moreover, the SBA puts a first lien position on all business assets over the seller, which requires them to subordinate their lien interest to the bank. Sound good if you're a seller? Nope. And it doesn't end there. In most cases, the seller can't accept any payments for two years.[55] Traditionally, seller financing would typically amortize for as short as one year and at most five, so the SBA effectively makes it so unattractive I rarely see it executed in SBA-backed acquisitions.

As of January 2018, the SBA does allow for partner buyouts. This is where one or more partners can buy out the other partner in a business. However, the borrower has to buy out 100 percent of the seller's ownership. Because all remaining partners in the business would be loan guarantors, the seller's ownership can only be bought

---

55   In instances where seller financing is approved, the buyer has to have a minimum of 10 percent cash in the purchase, and the SBA will review after two years to see if the seller can begin receiving payments.

on a pro-rata basis of all remaining partners. In other words, the terms that the SBA will loan in this instance does not play well with new acquisitions, so the company is more likely than not to change hands completely.

As a result, the deal structure restrictions SBA-backed loans require, end up putting more risk on the buyer by forcing them practically to acquire the business in full on day one. This means that asking the seller to put their money where their mouth is with a seller note or earnout is not a reasonable expectation, and the buyer is entering a secured commitment with the bank.

There is some silver lining to this, however: it simplifies the deal, makes the ongoing relationship with the seller clear cut, and gives the acquisition entrepreneur full ownership at closing.

Finally, speed is not a strength of government institutions, and SBA processing is no different. Bankers will look you right in the eye and tell you they can close a loan in thirty days. This doesn't typically happen. Ever. Usually it does take thirty days to get the loan approved, assuming communication is good. But because the SBA is a government institution, it's parallel to sending your loan application to the post office. Remember that I told you to find a preferred SBA lending bank? If you don't, you can easily lose an additional six weeks at this stage. A PLP lender, or someone who can process SBA loans faster than the rest, can typically close in forty-five days after the loan is approved.

It might not seem like a big deal out of context, but when a seller has decided to sell and you're the buyer, you'll want the deal closed as soon as possible so that you can be assured the business is being managed properly day to day. Time kills all deals, and adding six weeks at the end is critical. If the broker or seller suspects a hang up, they might start preparing second options behind you; and if they can get a verbal better offer, from a strategic buyer for example, it might incentivize them to throw your offer off course so they can execute that better offer. This is a risk, and you need to manage it early so you're not in a similar position later.

The best thing you can do as a potential buyer is be prepared by getting prequalified. This is the best avenue to assure you can execute in a timely manner.

SEARCH FUNDS

A note should be made on search funds as either an alternative to bank financing or to acquire a larger company. Search funds are attributed to being started by H. Irving Grousebeck,[56] a Stanford University professor and cofounder of the Stanford Center for Entrepreneurial Studies in 1984.

The concept is very similar to what we have been describing. The exception is that instead of utilizing bank financing to support your own efforts, the acquisition entrepreneur pools together private investors to, first, fund the search process, then invest in an acquisition once the target company is identified. It's much like running your own private equity firm or raising cash from angel investors for a startup.

Generally, search funds look for companies in the $5 million to $30 million price range—requiring $2 million to $10 million of equity infusion. According to *Forbes*, search funds prefer fragmented industries, sustainable market positions, a history of stable cash flows, have been "under managed" prior to the acquisition, and long-term opportunities for improvement and growth.[57] Essentially, a platform profile.

---

56   *https://www.searchfunder.com/searchfunds*

57   *https://www.forbes.com/sites/vanessaloder/2014/08/07/the-search-fund-model-how-to-become-a-twenty-six-year-old-ceo-if-youre-willing-to-kiss-frogs/#3ea4d0051190*

Search funds have grown in popularity as an alternative for typical MBA career paths. It allows for acquisition entrepreneurs to get started immediately after business school and with more capital. Because of the growing awareness and success of the model, *searchfunder.com* reports the number of search funds has increased 40 percent every year for the last five years.

Search funds are great ways to get additional capital and typically will look for the same things a bank does. But like any other investor group, you're going to need to court and manage investors, as well as give up equity.

PARTNERSHIPS

If you are working with a partner, be sure you have worked through who is going to do what, who is bringing what amount of capital to the deal, and be extremely clear on what you are looking for. In regard to the banking outreach and interviews, there may be one member spearheading the effort, but both will need the items outlined above in order to give banks what they are looking for.

As a longtime member of the Entrepreneur's Organization, I can share that a large number of issues entrepreneurs have relate to working through conflicts with a business partner. Having unclear, unwritten expectations or assumptions can result in misalignment, which takes the focus off progress. Having a good relationship with clear roles and responsibilities, and compensation attached to performance instead of ownership, can save a lot of headaches. You'll also want to consider getting buy-sell agreements in place.

OTHER PUNCH-LIST ITEMS

The bank will require you to carry key-man insurance[58] for the amount and term of the unsecured portion of your loan,[59] so you'll want to knock that out early. Engage an insurance company that your bank likes and get the process underway. It will require a medical checkup and determining how much you can be insured for. Don't buy the insurance yourself since this is a business expense that you can put into the company and get the tax benefit of.

Life insurance isn't just important for the bank but your family as well. If something happens to you, the insurance will pay off, at absolute minimum, the uncollateralized portion of the debt so the business can be operated or sold without having to worry about the loss of your involvement. If your family chooses to operate it, the total cash flow will increase either by eliminating the need for monthly loan payments altogether, or through increasing the cash benefit at exit with the equity buildup provided by the insurance.

HELOC stands for Home Equity Line of Credit. I seriously doubt you'll want to pull from something like this while having a secured bank loan on your business, but you never know if you'll need access to capital later. A HELOC is a loan on the equity portion of your home. The reason I bring this up is that once you have an SBA loan in place, you're unable to be approved for a HELOC, which ties up that equity until the SBA is paid back. I suggest you get approved for a HELOC from the bank that has your mortgage prior to closing on an SBA loan.

---

58   Key-man insurance refers to life insurance on the operator of the company. This assures them that if you die, the bank can get paid back. If you have a spouse, watch your back because they can get your company debt-free if something were to happen to you.

59   "Unsecured" in this instance could be the portion of the loan that is not backed by hard assets, or the portion of the loan that is not backed specifically by real estate. I have seen both instances.

That said, the bank may require you to close the HELOC if additional working capital is built into the loan or a Cap Line is in place. The reason is because they need to be able to monitor outside debt to know whether the borrower is becoming too leveraged. A borrower with a HELOC makes it hard for the bank to monitor that.

CPAs

You likely have a Certified Public Accountant (CPA) and lawyer you work with already, and they may or may not be the right people for your acquisition activity. CPAs can bring immense value to your review and understanding of a business, and lawyers are the number one leading source of deals that don't close. You want to be absolutely sure that you're getting into this process with the right professionals because they will have a significant impact on how your acquisition process goes, as well as its outcome.

When you are meeting with M&A Advisors and bankers, be sure to ask whether they have recommendations on CPAs and lawyers they like or have experience going through this process with. Make sure to ask for email referrals and call and meet with all of them. These will be the professionals who are used to this type of activity.

Accountants come in all shapes and sizes, and bookkeepers are very different from licensed CPAs. A good CPA can understand a business by looking at the history and comparing internal statements with tax returns. They understand business strategy and know where the snakes can hide in the grass in financial statements. They will be critical in helping you with due diligence later and asking the right questions. More importantly, they'll help identify where problems lie and can keep you out of trouble.

Some CPAs work at accounting firms that do little more than file corporate tax returns. You may find someone you want to work with there, but finding CPAs that engage in business transactions will give you an edge. They'll have experience knowing where their due diligence efforts have helped and how deals get done.

Some things to ask about include whether they have experience on both sides of the table—both representing a buyer and a seller. Asking what size transactions they have worked on is important because the small differences from $1 million to $50 million transactions will give insight on how they "believe" the process works. Ask whether they have a due diligence checklist or, if they were to make one, what would be on it. Finally, make sure they'll have time to commit when you need it. If you're wanting to close on May 1st this could put your due diligence period in the middle of tax time.

You'll want to discuss their fee structure up front as well. How they would charge for something like this, what they would expect to happen, how they can help, and what your expected cost will be. Like everything, this is negotiable, so make sure it's something you can live with. Often, I'll ask them to invoice the work after the close of the deal so that I can pay for it as a business expense and get the tax benefit.

CPAs are also privy to which business owners are considering selling. Be sure to share your target statement with them and see whether they have leads you can follow up with.

LAWYERS

Time and time again, lawyers are deal breakers and not deal makers. This is because their mission is to protect their client at all costs, even if it means the deal doesn't go through. Redline documents going back and forth will be the most sensitive time of the process. Everyone is emotional, stakes are high, and the lawyers get in the middle.

You, as the buyer, either want to get the deal done or you don't. You either trust the seller or you don't. If you don't trust the seller do not buy the company. If you don't want to buy the company, then walk away. But if you trust the seller and you want to buy the company, you are looking for documents that can help two responsible adults who want to get a deal done with a reasonable amount of protection.

I believe strongly that it is your responsibility to make sure you, not your lawyer, are comfortable where sacrifices in protection are made. They will accept the role of protecting you at all costs; you need to manage them or all you will have is a large legal bill and a promising deal that went south.

My first recommendation for managing lawyers is to start by communicating the above. Ask them for boiler plate documents (the M&A Advisor may be able to provide this as well, but understand that the Advisor in all circumstances represents the seller) that you can work. You'll want to use your lawyer's documents because they won't have to review the whole thing from top to bottom. This will keep your costs down. Also, the buyer is the one who wants the rights and warranties, whereas the seller doesn't want any, so utilizing the buyer's legal team's documents can put the buyer in the best position and limit the first round of back-and-forth.

Second, tell your lawyer what you want rather than letting them set the agenda. Asking for recommendations is absolutely fine and recommended but make the call and give them direction. You should avoid the buyer's lawyer and seller's lawyer talking on the phone and negotiating directly. Again, there are exceptions, and I have been in deals where a detail needed to get worked out and this was the best way to solve it; but typically, this is an example of two people who get paid high hourly rates discussing something they likely won't agree on easily.

I have been on the buying side where the M&A Advisor stepped to the side and let the lawyers work out the contracts. The deal was overly complicated, very expensive, delayed by almost a year, and the Advisor didn't have to work as hard as he should have.

Lawyer-to-lawyer deals are very common in the middle market when companies have attorneys on staff and they play a huge role in completing the agreements, but you will spend less money and get the deal closed—which is your goal—when you take a hands-on approach to managing your attorney.

I always negotiate a "not to exceed" budget with my attorney. This sets the limit for what will be spent throughout the course of the transaction. It's tough for them to agree due to unforeseen events, but I've had luck by setting assumptions and doing an ongoing review with them as the process continues. It's fair because natural risk of scope creep in projects like this. Taking this type of approach, though, results in communicating my budget goals and expectations. Like the CPA, I ask for the ability to pay after the deal has closed so I can take the tax benefit of treating it like a business expense.

REVIEWING LISTINGS

Don't forget you're beginning to review listings while meeting brokers. While reviewing listings, it's really about seeing what is interesting to you and what might hit your target statement.

Listings are just a general introduction to the opportunities available. It will typically tell just enough to either rule it out or interest you in getting more information. The vague overview will likely include descriptions of the revenue, SDE, industry, location, and a paragraph or two about the type of business it is, specifically pointing out the industry. Although the descriptions are vague, you've calculated what you can afford and you know your SDE goals for the acquisition, your minimum revenue goals, and the type of opportunity you're looking for. The purpose of reviewing listings is to reach out and look at everything—but be quick to decide it's not a fit. Talk to the brokers, explain your target statement, ask them to keep you in mind. Be proactive, telling them when listings profile businesses that don't match your goals.

Perhaps more important at this stage, you know your limiters. These will enable you to ignore listings that don't pass those basic requirements. Don't request more information on listings you can pass on easily and have limited motivation to buy.

Being able to pass quickly on things that aren't a fit will enable you to move forward just as quickly on opportunities that look good. As you start to move to the next step, requesting more information in the form of an Offering Memorandum from listing brokers, you will be asked to sign a non-compete. This is because the confidentiality involved with listing a business for sale puts a seller at extreme risk. Do not take advantage of this information in any way that might be questionable. Respect their property and their information and treat it as confidentially as you would want your information treated. To you, each of these listings is a potential purchase, but to the seller, it is their baby and they are proud and protective.

When you first request more information about a listing, you'll be asked to sign a confidentiality agreement before moving forward. Do not take this lightly. The seller is exposing tremendously valuable information, and you cannot take advantage of this information in any way other than reviewing the opportunity.

Once agreed to, you'll be given an Offering Memorandum that will outline the company in more detail. Typically, the location and name of the company and a comprehensive review of the business, including a write up about what they do, what industry they are in, and past financial performance. If the listing looks like it has potential to satisfy your goals, or has real interest for you, that you get to work quickly.

WHY ARE THEY SELLING?

Although this is a critical question and often asked early if not immediately by a potential buyer, I believe it is the most over-weighted question you'll ask the entire time. I bring this up because you will find that you will ask the broker this during a peripheral conversation, before the first seller call.

I will tell you now that they are selling because, when you own a business, the biggest return payday is in the exit. You will want this too, either three to five years down the road or at the end of your career. Their reason may be as simple as they are looking to retire or you may get a vague answer that sounds truthful but might be blocking an issue. They've done everything with the business that they can or they have a new opportunity they want to focus on, for example.

Does this mean they are trying to offload a company quickly because it's about to decline? It's certainly possible. This happens. You need to ask the question and evaluate what you think the true answer is. Ultimately, a quick review will tell you where their business is in the industry lifecycle and what you suspect is the outlook for the business. Through due diligence, research, and conversations with the seller, you'll identify what the risks inherent to opportunity are, and what your strengths can bring to the table.

Ultimately, that's what the acquisition entrepreneur decides for themselves and then chooses to go to work on the right opportunity. One opportunity that is passed on by one person might be exactly the right opportunity for you, and vice versa. But great listings go quickly, often resulting in a bidding war or, at least, high interest from potential buyers. Always be prudent, but if you like a listing make sure you jump on it and get to work immediately.

CHAPTER 7

BUY FOR THE FUTURE, PAY FOR THE PAST

IN THIS CHAPTER, WE'LL ADDRESS THE NUMBERS SURROUNDING a potential acquisition. Entire books and entire careers are built around understanding, analyzing, and projecting financial performance. Since we'll be spending one chapter on the topic, my goal is to give a brief overview of how cash flows through a company, understanding what the financial statements are telling you, and how to attach your own value to a company. As an acquisition entrepreneur, you're buying the company for the future, but you'll pay for the past. As a result, the initial goal is for you to understand what the business can afford to be bought for so that you can make an offer you are comfortable with.

Did you catch that?

Rule number one for establishing a purchase price is making sure *the business* can afford to pay for the business. So much of the first half of this book is focused on you as an entrepreneur, your skillsets, and what *you* can afford. When it comes time to acquiring a company, sure, you have to come up with the equity infusion; but as we've discussed, this down payment can be as little as 10 percent, or less if you're able to close without an SBA loan and negotiate seller financing.

INITIAL REVIEW

When you first request more information about a company and sign a confidentiality agreement, you'll be given an Offering Memorandum (OM), which will typically include two parts.

First, a write-up on the business including things like:

- asking price
- name
- location
- product or service offering
- number of employees
- who they are and their roles
- customer overview and concentration
- reason for selling
- typically, a growth plan for moving forward

Second, a report on financial performance, typically given in the form of recast income statements for the past two to five years and a current balance sheet.

The purpose of the OM is not to run complete due diligence on; rather, it's to give enough information about the company for the buyer to evaluate the opportunity and determine whether it's of real interest. If, after reviewing an OM, you do have interest in moving forward, the first step is going to be for you to have a call with the intermediary who listed the property and sell them on why you're a good buyer.

"*What?*" I hear you say, "*Why should I have to sell them? They are the ones who are trying to sell me something, shouldn't they be selling me?"*

We'll talk about this further in Chapter 8 when we discuss the seller, but for now let me share that this one attitude shift will take you from a cynical tire-kicker looking for excuses not to buy a company, to a problem-solving CEO who will be able to execute on your commitment to be an acquisition entrepreneur. There is a right time to be cynical, and it's in due diligence; but when engaging with M&A Advisors and sellers, I always suggest selling them on why you are a good buyer even if not for this specific opportunity. Remember, the broker here is the one with deal flow, and they are always looking for "good" buyers that they want to work with.

When reviewing the financial performance in the OM, you'll go through various steps. First, you'll just want to get familiar with the business. Second, you'll want to analyze, and third, if you get this far, you'll want to project the future performance.

To get started, I want you to completely forget about the listing price of the company (if it has one, the larger the deal the more likely it's listed without a price). Sure, it's a benchmark that you can take into consideration later. For now, just know that it's an estimate of value that may or may not be right for you. Privately held companies do not have one firm valuation. There is a range of value determined by the growth of the company, the earnings of the company, current market conditions, level of competition, and a host of other variables. You're going to reverse engineer what the business is worth to you, because that's the only valuation that matters.

We're going to walk you step-by-step through how to evaluate a business starting with the basics, then moving into the financial statements. Finally, we'll look at the different ways to value a business. In the end, you'll be paying for the past performance of the company, with the goal of growing it from there. As a result, you'll be paying a price the company can afford so that you can make money as you build value. So, let's dive in.

THE BASICS

I'm going to assume you are not an accounting expert. You do not have to be one, so don't let this stop you from acquiring a company. The numbers tell a story about what has happened in the past, describing the overall health and performance of the company. However, business is not all about accounting. It's just one piece of the puzzle. Do not be intimidated. Accounting is a skill that can be acquired.

Once you own a company, you'll learn more and more about accounting (you'll have to). In the meantime, this is a skill that you can get assistance with from your accountant, the internal accounting team of the company you're acquiring, or a bookkeeper.

When business schools survey their alumni and the greater business community, the top ranked skillset that upper managers claim they wish to improve is accounting and finance. The irony, of course, is if they had focused in accounting and finance they'd be accountants and not upper management. Accounting becomes more important as you begin to walk down the business path—but accounting is not the driver of value, it is the reporting mechanism for what happened. Improved knowledge will come in time.

During the acquisition process, you'll lean on accounting professionals regardless of your skill level, since two sets of eyes are always better than one—especially if the second set is a CPA. We're going to give you a very simplified overall framework here so you can get your sea legs under you and get familiar with the business you are reviewing.

In due diligence, you will spend considerable time determining the accuracy of the information you have been given, including financial information. For the original review, you'll just want to assume that everything being presented is accurate. There are two main reasons for this. First, good brokers understand that inaccurate information in their OMs will typically result in buyers not trusting the rest of the opportunity either. Discovering inaccurate financial information after a business has been placed under a Letter of Intent to purchase is probably one of the worst things that can happen to a deal. A valuable intermediary will take the time up front to prepare the information appropriately.

Obviously, the quality of the listing intermediary and their internal process for putting together OMs and recast statements will have a lot to do with that; but for now, you can move forward believing what's been outlined in the OM is relatively accurate, knowing you'll have plenty of time to validate later. In other words, keep the "numbers don't lie" axiom top of mind during initial review. You'll have plenty of time to evaluate how the numbers were figured later.

ACCRUAL VS. CASH BASIS ACCOUNTING

Before we review the outline of financial statement that will likely be provided, let's back up and consider how cash moves through a company.

Let's say a product is sold from the company to a customer in January. In order for the product to be delivered, materials to make that finished product were bought in December. The company has thirty days to pay for the materials, but if they pay early they get a discount. The customer has thirty days to pay for the product, but they take forty-five to do so.

So, here's what just happened. The company spends X dollars in December so they can buy materials at a discount (in order to increase their margins). They sold the product in January, got paid for it in March (because the customer paid in forty-five days), and all the while you paid employee salaries six times between paying for the materials and getting paid for the product.

Sounds a little confusing right? This is why most businesses will keep what's called "accrual basis" accounting. This style of accounting allows the sale to be recorded as revenue in January, as well as the costs associated with that sale. It allows for the sale dollars and the expenses associated with that sale to be matched together.

This is important to understand, because managing the cash flow of a business can be one of the toughest things to learn due to the opacity of how cash moves through a business—especially at times of growth. Cash being the "oxygen" of an organization is ultimately what you'll absolutely need to get a rhythm for as the CEO, and studying the financial statements is what will get you there.

Conversely, "cash basis" accounting would record the material expenses for this order in December, when it was paid, and the revenue in March, when it was received. To make the situation even more confusing while evaluating potential acquisitions, most companies, as we've pointed out, keep an accrual-based accounting internally for their records, but file their taxes on a cash-based model. This results in the internal statements and tax returns often not matching, simply because they tell time differently. The company's accountant likely performs a reconciliation between the two, and guess what? So will yours in the due diligence phase.

Why would companies keep accrual-based records internally but cash basis when filing taxes? The reason is that accrual-based accounting typically provides better insight to how the company is actually performing on a month-to-month basis, but taxes can be one of the largest expenses a company pays in any given year, and smart business owner will do everything they can to lower non-operational expenses like taxes. Cash-based accounting will typically allow lower tax expenses by delaying what is owed, which also adds a layer of protection for the owner.

There are many benefits of accrual-based accounting, not the least of which is insight into accounts receivable (AR) and accounts payable (AP). When materials are bought but not yet paid for, the invoiced amount will be filed under AP. In the same regard, when items are sold but the cash has not been collected, it is filed under AR. This means that you, as the potential buyer, can review the statements knowing what is owed to suppliers and what is expected to be received from customers. Cash-based accounting does not have the same transparency, meaning you wouldn't have insight to what was owed to suppliers, nor what was owed to the company. So, step one is to make sure you know if the statements you are reviewing are on a cash basis or accrual basis.

HOW HEALTHY IS THE BUSINESS?

According to the Federal Reserve Bank of Chicago's Small Business Financial Health Analysis,[60] 88 percent of poor and below-average financially healthy businesses have revenues under $1 million. This is one of the reasons I don't often consider companies under this level of revenue for a first acquisition. So the first thing you want to do is determine whether the company you are reviewing is financially healthy or not.

---

60 *https://www.frbsf.org/community-development/files/small-business-financial-health-analysis.pdf*

As you begin to review financial performance and statements, there are five areas of specific importance you'll be wanting to look into: revenue, profit, operational efficiency, cash flow, and the total Owner Benefit (the SDE). All of this information can be found in their financial statements provided in the OM.

There are three standard financial statements: the balance sheet, the income statement, and the statement of cash flows. The good news is that financial statements follow the same general format across all companies, so the learning curve doesn't start over every time. If you haven't had a lot of exposure to financial statements in the past, publicly traded companies have financial statement readily available, simply jump online and start reviewing the financials of your favorite companies to start getting familiar. You can also check out the price-to-earnings (PE) ratios and compare them to the multiple you'll be paying for a lower middle-market company.[61] Although large, publicly traded companies and privately owned, lower middle-market companies are completely different, it can offer perspective on how the two classes are valued.

THE BALANCE SHEET

The balance sheet is a snapshot of a company's assets and liabilities and the owner's equity from a specific date, such as the day that ends a month, quarter, or year. It paints a portrait of what a company owns, what it owes, and the net value to the shareholders or members.

Balance sheets are broken out on two sides.[62] The left side reflects the assets of the company, while the right side contains

---

61   Investors in public companies might try to get a 3 percent income-to-value return after inflation. As an acquisition entrepreneur, you'll be expecting closer to 30 percent.

62   Sometimes presented in a top and bottom format, rather than left and right.

both the liabilities and owner's equity. The balance sheet is named such because the two sides must balance by always reverting to the following formula:

Assets = Liabilities + Owner's Equity

An even simpler calculation would be to acknowledge that assets, those things of value owned by the company, minus the liabilities, those things owed by the company, equals the value of the company to the ownership at a certain point in time, or its "book value." This is the essence of the balance sheet.

For example, let's say the company takes out a seven-year, $50,000 loan to purchase a widget-making machine. When they close on the loan, the liability side of the balance sheet, specifically the long-term notes payable, will increase by $50,000. Simultaneously, the asset side of the balance sheet increases with a brand new $50,000 widget-making machine.[63] Over time, the loan will get paid down and the owner's equity will increase with the value of the equity in the machine.

ASSETS

A balance sheet's assets can be indented in two categories, current assets and long-term assets. Since a balance sheet is recorded in order by most liquid to least liquid, or the ease in which it can be converted into cash, the current assets will be listed first.

Current assets include very liquid items like cash and equivalents, any marketable securities, accounts receivable, inventory, and

---

63 At the risk of getting lost in the weeds, I left out that depending on how the machine was acquired, cash might first increase by $50,000, followed by cash decreasing by $50,000, with the increase in value of machinery.

prepaid expenses. Long-term assets reflect assets owned by the company that are harder to convert into cash—items like illiquid investments; fixed assets like buildings, land, or the widget-making machine example above; as well as accumulated depreciation and intangible assets. Intangible assets include things like software that was developed by the company, patents or certain intellectual property, and goodwill.

Let's unpack a few of these terms.

DEPRECIATION

Depreciation is an accounting tool that allows companies to devalue assets over their useful life. Let's take the widget-making machine example above. This machine is not expected to last forever. Let's say the predicted useful life is ten years—that's how long it's expected to be operational before it needs to be replaced. Therefore, its value at the end of ten years is $0.00, which means it is valued at $50,000 today and will be worth $0.00 in ten years.

By deducting $5,000 per year for ten years, the financial statements are able to capture the lesser value of the equipment as it ages over time. Since depreciation is a non-cash expense, meaning it doesn't actually cost the company $5,000 out of operational income every year, it is recorded as an asset. Non-cash expenses can be a little tricky to learn but it's an important concept for the acquisition entrepreneur. We'll come back to depreciation later in the chapter as it applies to calculating true cash flow.

INTELLECTUAL PROPERTY

Intellectual property is an interesting one. Since there is no marketplace for IP or custom-built software, for example, it's tough to value. As a buyer, I typically devalue this substantially. Here's why:

the value of IP is in its ability to generate earnings for the company. If your IP is ownership of the brand "Coca-Cola," that IP's ability to generate sales is undeniable, because of its ability to earn sales revenue and, subsequently, profits. If the IP is a software that someone invested $500,000 in to build but it generates no revenue, should it be valued at $500,000? As a buyer of a company with established revenue, infrastructure, and earnings, you are buying cash flow, not non-revenue generating IP. Non-revenue generating IP is typically referred to as a "startup looking for funding."[64] Instead, you, as an acquisition entrepreneur, will be looking to acquire a company's infrastructure only so far as its ability to generate cash flow.

GOODWILL

Goodwill is an intangible asset that represents the value over and above the value of the hard assets. For example, let's say a dropshipping based, eCommerce company with no real estate, inventory, or assets of any kind generates $250,000 in earnings every year for the owner. When the company is bought for $800,000 (3.2 multiple on $250,000), where is the value booked? In goodwill. Goodwill can also be referred to as a "customer list" or any other intangible asset name that was acquired at a premium over asset value.

LIABILITIES

Liabilities headline the right side of the balance sheet and outline what the company owes. Here's where the debts will be found for bank loans, equipment purchases, lines of credit, as well as accounts

---

64 To be clear, I am not discouraging startups looking for funding to build software or any other infrastructure. Billions of dollars have been made doing just this. However, it is not the focus of the acquisition entrepreneur and that is the reason a potential buyer will significantly devalue non-revenue-generating IP in this example.

payable, rent, tax, utilities, and any customer prepayments will be listed. It's obviously critical to understand in detail all the debts of a company.

OWNER'S EQUITY

Owner's equity is calculated simply by taking the value of the total assets and subtracting the total liabilities. Depending on the size and structure of the company, this can be referred to as "owner's equity," "shareholder's equity," or "net equity." The equity portion of the balance sheet is broken down by retained earnings and capital stock. Retained earnings being the amount of earnings retained inside the company from prior years, and capital stock referring to how much each owner paid for their share of ownership in the company.

A MOMENT IN TIME

You can learn a lot about the overall health of the company by analyzing the balance sheet. It's common to look at ratios like Return on Equity (ROE);[65] and debt to equity, the quick ratio to measure liquidity;[66] and Current Ratio, which is current assets divided by current liabilities. These help identify the return owners are getting from the business, how much leverage is being used to operate, and the ability to pay off short-term obligations.

Because the balance sheet is a snapshot of a company's financial position at a moment in time, it's not the best tool for extracting trends playing out. Balance sheets are best analyzed as presenting

---

65 ROE is calculated by taking the earnings from the income statement (next section) and dividing by the average of owner's equity on the balance sheet.

66 Quick ratio is (Cash + AR + Short Term Investments) / Current Liabilities and is commonly thought to represent working capital because it eliminates inventory. When projecting working capital, also consider three months of operating expenses for comparison.

a moment in time so they can be compared to balance sheets from other periods in time, or perhaps more importantly, to other businesses in the same industry.

One important metric you can pull from the comparative balance sheet is the Cash Conversion Cycle, which is insightful when determining how long the time is from when inventory is purchased and when the cash is collected from the sale. Take the amount of days inventory is outstanding and add it to the days sales are outstanding, then divide by payables outstanding. If revenue stays level, this will be your tied up working capital. If you grow, however, you better understand how to fund this period of time where the cash is tied up.

THE INCOME STATEMENT

While the balance sheet is a snapshot of a specific date, the income statement reports a company's financial performance over a specific period of time, whether that be monthly, quarterly, or annually. Commonly referred to as the profit and loss statement (P&L), the income statement provides all revenue and expenses of a company during that period and reports whether the company is profitable or not.

The top line of the income statement is for incoming sales or revenue, while the bottom line is the net income. In between are the expenses subtracted from revenue to get to the net income (or loss). You're likely familiar with the common adage, "What's the bottom line?" This refers directly to the net income (typically marked with a double bottom line).

Personally, I like to split the income statement into two parts. The first is getting from revenue to gross margin, and the second is going from gross margin to net income.

THE TOP LINE

The first part is fairly straightforward. It starts with revenue, which should be all revenue from all sources: product sales, consulting services, even interest income. These are typically broken out by category or product line. Total revenue, or sales, are commonly referred to as the top line.

COST OF GOODS SOLD

Following revenue is the cost of goods sold (COGS). COGS is the direct costs attributable to the specific goods sold. In other words, it matches the revenue reported with the material and direct labor costs associated with that revenue. For example, if a company resells innovative bathroom products and they sold 150 toilets in a given month, the cost of goods sold would be just the 150 toilets that were sold in that month—not the entire truck of toilets that they purchased (the non-sold inventory would be found on the balance sheet).

COGS is generally "variable costs," or costs that occur only when something is sold. Subtracting the COGS from revenue results in the gross margin.

GROSS MARGIN

Gross margin captures exactly the concept of "I bought these candy bars for $1.00 and I sold them for $3.00." The revenue for each candy bar is $3.00, while the COGS is $1.00 (33 percent), making the gross margin, $2.00 (67 percent). It's the profit gained by reselling the materials and adding the value the company delivers (in the case of the candy bars, likely convenience or accessibility).

The big takeaway from looking at gross margin is that, assuming COGS can't be reduced, this margin really represents 100 percent of the cash available for the balance of the operating expenses and the resulting net profit. Think of it this way: if you could eliminate 100 percent of all operational expenses, this would be the maximum amount of cash you could capture during the time period presented. In the candy bar example, gross margin is 67 percent of each unit sold (which is absolutely at the higher end of gross margins, by the way). The higher the gross margin the healthier the company. This is because a higher gross margin allows for unwanted fluctuations in revenue and/or high reinvestment opportunities into the company. Understanding what a typical gross margin percentage is in an industry you're analyzing is important because gross margins as a percentage vary drastically by industry.

OPERATING EXPENSES

Operating expenses fall below gross margin on the income statement and largely represent fixed expenses. There might be some variance based on sales level (additional inventory charges or sales commissions, for example), but they largely represent the overhead associated with a business, or costs that must be met every month. Because expenses are what reduce the profitability of the company, managing operating expenses will be one of the critical things you as the leader will do. The income statement is where they are recorded. Expenses are typically broken down into five categories: selling, general, and administrative (SGA); depreciation and amortization; other expenses; interest expense; and taxes. Net income is presented on the infamous "bottom line" after all the expenses are taken from the gross margin dollars. Net income is the profit that can be used for reinvestment in the company or additional cash to the ownership.

EARNINGS

But wait! Does net income really represent the cash generated by the business? It really doesn't, and here's why: depreciation and amortization are what's called "non-cash" expenses.

We discussed accumulated depreciation on the balance sheet, but on the income statement we'll see the amount of depreciation associated with that period deducted as an expense. However, there was no actual cash subtracted. If your car is worth $35,000 January 1st and $27,000 on December 31st of the same year, you didn't actually spend the difference, you just lost value. The IRS allows this depreciation to be subtracted as an expense from the net income so that you do not need to pay taxes on those dollars that were invested in the equipment in the first place.

Amortization works the same as depreciation but is applied to intangible assets like goodwill. So, you can actually take depreciation and amortization and add it back to net earnings to discover the cash generated in addition to what's reported on net income. Principal payments paid on debt, however, are not expensed by a company. A business with interest payments will clearly have principal payments as well. You'll need to subtract the principal to understand the current true cash flow of the company.

However, to understand the cash the company has generated *as a result of its operations*, analysts will calculate the company's Earnings Before taking out Interest, Taxes, Depreciation, and Amortization. This is creatively called EBITDA. It's not a line item on the income statement, but you can quickly calculate it with the information available. We'll be revisiting this number when we look at valuation later in the chapter, but in the meantime, understand that the M&A Advisor who put together the OM for the business you are reviewing will have calculated this at the bottom of the income statement. As an aside, a company's EBITDA is the number that publicly traded companies commonly place their value on.

I've been asked why EBITDA contains taxes in it. After all, it's a real expense that the company had to pay. The answer, I believe, is because a company could choose to increase capital expenditures in order to increase depreciation and interest enough that it could report no net income at all, pay zero taxes, and have a large amount of non-cash expenses to thank for it. On the flip side, a company could shun investing in new equipment, have no depreciation or amortization, and have the maximum tax expense. Either way, it's a management decision that can be standardized by adding back all these factors. It allows for comparisons from one company to the next as an apples to apples comparison, because, ultimately, EBITDA points to the company's ability to make money regardless of how you finance operations.

In companies that are actively for sale in the true lower middle market, under, say, $20 million in revenue (all the way down to a Main Street business like a laundromat or car wash) additional Owner Benefit or Owner Discretionary earnings are added back as well. We'll go through this line by line when we look at valuation, but for now just understand that the Seller Discretionary Earnings(SDE) is a calculation of all discretionary earning the owner of the business had during this period. It might include items like salary, benefits, automobiles, or even one-time expenses that were at the discretion of the owner. The OM will calculate this below the EBITDA calculation on the income statement so that you get a true sense of the total value of the company to the owner during this period.

Alright, we got a little bit into the analysis side there, but it's important to understand what you're being shown on the income statement—an internal document, tax return, or contained in an Offering Memorandum.

CASH FLOW STATEMENT

The third major financial statement is the statement of cash flow. This statement reports the cash at the beginning of a period, the cash at the end of a period, and the cash in and cash out that impacted the difference. It merges operating results that you would find on the income statement with the changes in the balance sheet in one place.

Remember how the income statement is likely reported on an accrual basis? This means the income reported on the income statement is not the same as the cash position. The cash flow statement is a snapshot into the cash flow management of the firm, reflecting the overall liquidity, understanding where the cash in the company is going, and helping to assess the short-term viability of a company (i.e. can it pay its bills).

Cash flow statements are sometimes provided in an OM, typically on larger-sized deals, but it's not common. You'll typically see this during due diligence. The purpose of the cash flow statement is for a potential buyer to understand the working capital demands of the business, and to make sure the company is producing enough cash to pay its expenses.

Adding additional working capital funds to a bank loan for an acquisition is commonplace. If you are utilizing the SBA, the working capital can be acquired with a minimum of 10 percent down, which can be a great way to apply inexpensive financing.

FURTHER ANALYSIS

The statements provide the reports you need to evaluate the financial profile of the company. However, you need to create your own spreadsheet and recreate all the financial statements yourself. This provides two benefits: first, you will learn the business intimately as you enter in each number, processing what percent of revenue it is and noticing anomalies; second, it provides the information in your own spreadsheet for financial analysis and modeling. You'll want to analyze the past, but also project the future. Having your own spreadsheet will provide that.

When analyzing revenue, the best exercise you can do is a year-over-year comparison. This will show you the revenue trend of the company. If there were unusual occurrences of high revenue, this will also help to identify these and to remember to ask the seller about them later. Graph this so that you can visually see the trend. Ultimately, you are looking at monthly revenue for the year, or rolling twelve months, over the prior period(s).

OMs will typically include an income statement presented monthly (if not, you should request them). A great exercise to help understand how cash moves through a company is to take the last twelve months, then project them forward, applying your debt service, compensation, and any planned reinvestment to the model. This is a great way to really understand blips in expenses, the impact of any seasonality, and how the company will look in the future.

The OM will also likely highlight any customer concentration or revenues coming from a single customer or a few customers. The rule of thumb is that no customer is greater than 10 percent of revenues. If this is not the case, you'll need to intimately understand the relationship and value provided to that customer because it adds an element of risk to your acquisition.

An additional calculation that measures a company's productivity is revenue per employee. The higher the number, the more the company is doing with less expense. This is a great tool for understanding how efficient a business is simply because it's typical for the largest expense to be labor. Leveraging the people inside the company to execute more efficiently makes for a healthy company.

Conversely, many smaller companies are in the business of not paying taxes. Small business accountants regularly recommend buying equipment before the end of the year to lower profits and decrease the tax burden. This is a big difference from publicly traded companies where the stock price is commonly attached to quality and growth or profits. This is why calculations like EBITDA and SDE are more important in lower middle market and Main Street companies.

You'll also want to understand a certain company in light of its industry. Getting benchmarks from industry reports and online research are key to understanding how a company is doing within the realm in which it's playing.

THE CRITICAL FACTOR

One thing I need to underscore is, a lot of common financial analysis comes from potential investors analyzing past corporate performance to make predictions for future performance. When you are an acquisition entrepreneur, there is a critical piece of the story that is not apparent in common ratios or analysis—you. When you are analyzing past performance, it's important to understand that this performance is what happened under the current owner's management. If the results are good, what happens when they leave? What is their skillset? How, exactly are they getting these results and how can you make sure you keep those great parts performing?

Further, what will the business look like under your management? The ROE, debt to equity, and revenue per employee, for example, will all be different. How will you change it? Where can you improve? It is not common for lower middle-market companies to run these types of analysis on their business and you likely will have gained insights that current ownership many or may not have. Or perhaps you're planning on hiring a manager and simply taking a great return on your investment. These are all critical differences to keep in mind when looking at a business to acquire because common financial analysis rules of thumb don't always apply. You'll have to question what is important in your circumstance.

VALUATION

Valuing a privately held company can be as complicated as you make it. Ultimately, there is a value to the buyer and a value to the seller, and getting the two parties to agree on a transaction usually means that both parties are getting most of what's important to them out of the deal.

The most common ways to value a company are asset based and cash flow based. It's important to understand them, even if they're not applicable, so that you can begin to understand how others apply or calculate approximate value.

ASSET-BASED VALUATION

There are three main asset-based valuations: book value (BV), fair market value (FMV), and liquidation value (LV).

BOOK VALUE

Book value we discussed earlier while reviewing the balance sheet. It's the net worth of the company as reported by its financial statement under owner's equity. It applies the value of the assets currently on the books, then subtracts the liabilities. This can be an interesting academic understanding, but in my experience, it's not at all accurate.

This is for two primary reasons. First, depreciated assets are being depreciated linearly over time on the books, but we all know that hard assets depreciate exponentially. We're all aware that a new car loses approximately 10 percent of its value the second you buy it from the dealer. However, the government classifies any company vehicle under 6,000 pounds in weight as a "luxury" automobile and applies restrictions to the rate of depreciation. This essentially ensures any book value would not match what the installation truck could be sold for on the open market. Ever try to sell a three-year-old computer? How about a short-run perfect binding machine without an in-line cutter?

We've discussed that the assets are only as good as their ability to produce earnings, and this is the second reason book value doesn't apply for you. As a buyer, what you are really interested in is the cash flow that is generated by the business. The infrastructure is simply the existing vehicle that creates those earnings. The other asset-based valuation methods do the same thing—attempt to apply an accurate value on the assets of the company.

FAIR MARKET VALUE

Fair market value addresses the issue that the value of the assets on the books is probably in error. There are professionals for hire who will evaluate the condition and attempt to calculate an estimated value of all the assets on the open market, should each asset be sold off individually. This type of analysis will discount accounts receivable that may or may not be in question, use the cash balance to simulate paying off payables or any liabilities, address value to current inventory levels, and apply useful life analyses on furniture and equipment.

Fair market value analysis is worthwhile if you are buying an asset-intensive business. It will help you understand what you are buying and help you identify what is and isn't useful to you moving forward. There may be pieces of equipment that you don't believe will be needed in the future and you can use the FMV of those items as negotiating points later. However, remember that FMV does not reflect the ability of these assets to generate cash flow. If assets do not generate cash flow than you won't be considering the company anyway unless you are looking for an undervalued turn around opportunity. If that's the case, you might be more interested in the company's liquidation value.

LIQUIDATION VALUE

Liquidation value estimates what all the assets in a company would sell for in a fire sale, then subtracts any outstanding liabilities. Essentially, if the company were to liquidate today in order to turn everything into cash, how much cash could it generate? This is the lowest possible value a company could have and is experienced only in occurrences of bankruptcy auctions. LV is an important calculation for turn-around experts looking to acquire underutilized opportunities, but you won't see any Offering Memorandums highlighting liquidation values.

CASH FLOW BASED VALUATION

Cash flow based valuation has two common methods: Discounted Cash Flow (DCF) and Valuation Multiple.

DISCOUNTED CASH FLOW

Discounted Cash Flow is the most common valuation method for transactions at investment banks. The approach starts with projecting the future earnings of a company by looking at prior history, industry projections, and a dozen assumptions, then discounting those future earnings by applying a weighted average cost of capital to a value that it would be worth today.

It's great in theory because it's attempting to apply a valuation on future cash flow, but in practice it's an academic exercise that is full of assumptions and significantly more effective in large, publicly traded firms, or, more specifically, eternally profitable, cash-cow type companies.

The formula typically looks something like this:

$$PV = CF1/(1+r) + CF2/(1+r)^2 + \ldots [TCF/(r\text{-}g)]/(1+k)^{n\text{-}1}$$

But don't worry, this isn't that book. This is typically something that you will learn in business school, but like all good complicated math, there is a shortcut that get extremely close to the result of using a DCF model for determining value.

VALUATION MULTIPLE

It didn't take long for markets to determine that all these valuation models result in some kind of multiple applied to a metric in the business in anticipation of capturing a certain return of invested dollars.

We've discussed EBITDA and SDE (or Adjusted EBITDA), which represent the cash flow of a company over the prior years to the shareholders or owner. Markets change all the time, but most Main Street businesses will sell for 2–3 × SDE, while most lower middle-market companies under $5 million in transaction value will sell for 2.5–6, depending on a number of factors. These factors include growth of the business, earnings of the business, growth of the industry, transferability of the business to new ownership, brand recognition, or other intangible assets.

Sometime multiples are applied to gross margins or revenue instead of earnings numbers, but typically, for acquisition entrepreneurs, that's a metric that won't apply for your transaction. After all, you're paying for the earnings, not the revenue.

The reason intermediaries, sellers, and buyers all like applying multiples is frankly because it's easy to do and it's easy to understand. For example, if a company is producing $600,000 in cash flow and you can acquire it for 3.5 times that, or $2,100,000, then you understand you are paying a price reflective of what the company produced over the prior three years and six months.

Determining what the SDE is and what the multiple should be is the trick. OMs will have suggested asking prices based on comparable companies that sold recently. The comps should take into consideration industry, growth rate, and earnings size, but you can't assume this is what the listing advisor did; only the best do this. Valuation is not an exact mathematical calculation based on research; you need to calculate what the business is worth to you.

FINANCIAL VALUE DRIVERS

Each business will have a value to you specifically. If a business's growth plan requires your skillset, does not contain any of your limiters, is something you can get genuinely excited about, and the business can afford to pay for itself, it's already a great fit.

But let's ignore all of that for a minute and look at a hypothetical exercise so you can experience how fluctuations in certain numbers impact the value of a company. Take a look at the three companies outlined below and try to decide which one is worth more.

(in 000s)	COMPANY 1	COMPANY 2	COMPANY 3
Revenue	$ 1,000	$ 1,000	$ 2,000
COGS	$ 700	$ 300	$ 1,200
Gross Margin	$ 300	$ 700	$ 800
Op. Expenses	$ 200	$ 600	$ 700
Net Income	$ 100	$ 100	$ 100

The top line shows the revenue of the different companies. This is all you'd learn at a cocktail party, by the way. The guy running the $2 million in revenue company is infamous for his success. Everyone at the party know that his company is worth more, right? In fact, it might be. With higher revenue he could attract the attention of bigger buyers when it comes time for him to exit.[67] The other entrepreneurs running Companies 1 and 2 will wonder what they can do to double their company's size, which is the right question—but we can see here in comparing one company to another, they have significantly different expense profiles.

Company 1 has a 30 percent gross margin on sales, while Company 2 has 70 percent; that's a big range. Company 3 comes in at 40 percent.

What Company 2 makes up in higher percentages of gross margin, and what Company 3 earns in higher dollar value of gross margin, they lose in operating expenses. Company 1, meanwhile, is running very lean in comparison to the others, and all three net incomes result in the same $100,000.

Ask yourself: which one is worth more?

Are they worth the same since the net income is the same?

This is where Seller's Discretionary Earnings comes into play.

---

67   This is a perfect example of how people looking at revenue during a search can be misleading. All three of these companies have the same net income, and yet only one of them would attract more potential buyers due to revenue alone.

(in 000s)	COMPANY 1	COMPANY 2	COMPANY 3
Revenue	$ 1,000	$ 1,000	$ 2,000
COGS	$ 700	$ 300	$ 1,200
Gross Margin	$ 300	$ 700	$ 800
Op. Expenses	$ 200	$ 600	$ 700
Net Income	$ 100	$ 100	$ 100
Add-Backs	$ 50	$ 250	$ 150
SDE	$ 150	$ 350	$ 250

After calculating EBITDA and any Owner Benefits, each company is able to apply the add-backs to the net income to give a more complete picture of the total cash flow to the current owner.

Company 2 has a higher SDE number, so it has a higher valuation than the others, right? That should be correct. Growth and earnings drive value in companies and Company 2 wins here with more earnings. If you apply the same multiple to each company, you'll see that Company 2 is worth considerably more in the marketplace.

(in 000s)	COMPANY 1	COMPANY 2	COMPANY 3
SDE	$ 150	$ 350	$ 250
Multiple	3	3	3
Valuation	$ 450	$ 1,050	$ 750

More importantly, Company 2 is financially worth more to the owner than Company 3 is to its owner during this specific period of time. Keep in mind that industry, competition, and growth rates can all impact the multiple used. A great online SAAS business at this revenue level could push a multiple twice as high today, while a declining company in a low profit and commodity industry might sell for below two times SDE. It all depends.

Valuation multiples are rarely applied to a single year like the above example. Instead, they will look at the prior three to five years and apply more weight to the more recent years. For example, the most recent year would be weighted 70 percent, the year prior 30 percent, and the third year back 10 percent.

Given the fluctuation in applied valuation models, it's critical to determine what the business is worth to *you*, not the marketplace. Let's take Company 2 as an example. Would you pay three-times for a business cash flowing $350,000 in Owner Benefit? Let's calculate the total transaction value first.

The most recent year had an SDE of $350,000, the year prior had $310,000, and the year before that was $275,000. You calculate a weighted average of $335,000 over the last three years and multiply it by three to get $1,005,000.

Let's say it's a service business so it has no inventory. Accounts receivable is sitting at $125,000 and accounts payable is only at $25,000, so there's $100,000 in working capital you'd have to purchase; and after running analysis, you decide you require another $75,000 for the upcoming busy season, closing costs, and legal and accounting fees associated with the close. You take this additional $175,000 and add it to the valuation you've calculated.

$1,005,000 + $175,000 = $1,180,000 total transaction

You decide to inject 10 percent equity to maximize your ROI, so you plan to put down $118,000 at closing and take on $1,062,000 in debt financing.

You use a loan calculator you downloaded from the app store to determine that $1,062,000 over ten years at 6 percent will cost $11,790 per month. You know that the company has been producing $29,167 in cash flow in the average month, which leaves about $208,000 for you to either take a salary (or hire a manager) or reinvest in the company. You've determined the company can afford to pay for itself, which is part of the puzzle, so you know the asking price is fine in that regard.

You also calculate that a $335,000 return on a $118,000 investment is a 283 percent annual ROI, which you are happy with. But you also understand it's not all cash, so you decide to calculate the ROI on your projected $150,000 salary, which will produce a 127 percent ROI. You also understand this assumes no growth in the business—and you're not going to buy a company you can't grow.

In ten years' time, you will have paid yourself $1.5 million in salary and paid off the bank loan so that you now run the company with zero debt. You've also managed to grow it 8 percent every year since you found a business whose growth plan needed your skillset. It's now exceeding $2 million in revenue and the total Owner Benefit to you is 17 percent, or over $350,000 a year.

You've determined you can service the debt, pay yourself a livable wage, and keep reserves to grow the business. From a financial perspective, this transaction is looking quite favorable.

SDE ANALYSIS

Calculating EBITDA is pretty straightforward, but it's critical when you review an opportunity that you go line by line through the add-backs. There are best practices on how to think about what to add back but this is where listing brokers can take liberties at your expense.

Typically, you'll see the owner's salary and benefits, but you'll also see listings of items that were simply perks to the owner. It's important to understand that many business owners know that any expense they can legitimately run through a business will reduce their taxes. As a result, you'll see cell phones and vehicles, and you just want to validate anything in this category.

The other add-back will be in nonrecurring expenses that occurred during the period. Often, these are things like heightened legal and accounting fees to manage a specific event that occurred, or the build out of a static website. You can also often find various advertising expenses in this category that may or may not be legitimate. Make sure you understand every one of them, and if you can't agree with it because you expect it will be an expense for you as well, take it out of your calculation.

YOUR VALUE VERSUS ASKING PRICE

Once you determine your own value on the opportunity, you now want to consider the asking price.

Entrepreneurs are notorious for overvaluing their companies. Trust me, this is the number one benefit you have going through a company that is already for sale. The M&A Advisor has already worked with the seller, sometimes for years, to get them mentally prepared in regard to what to expect. The asking price on a listing, given a good advisor, is likely a fair price and in the appropriate range for the business' value. More importantly, a seller will be thinking the price is somewhat accurate. Just like when you list your house for sale, it will either sell for a little under, full price, or a little above if it's a great property with high demand. Business listings are no different.

Of course, some brokers will try to get a listing simply by telling the seller they can sell a company at an overvalued price. If that's the case, you are now armed to determine that and will know when to walk way. If the company's past performance can't afford to cover the debt service to acquire it without additional growth, you're not paying for the past, you're paying for future growth.

Instead, let the future value of the business be the driver of your interest, then price that future value on past performance. This will

assure the value you build in the company will be yours to enjoy.
If you believe the company can be acquired in the correct price
range and that the company can provide long-term value to you in
the future, then you are in a good enough position at this point to
move forward with meeting the seller.

CHAPTER 8

THE SELLER'S JOURNEY

AFTER MY LAST ACQUISITION, THE BANKER SUPPLYING THE SBA loan told me, "Walker, my first job is to convince the prospective borrowers that we are absolutely the right bank for them, my second job is to then determine whether the loan is a good fit for the bank or not."

His comment rang true for me because this is exactly how I approach new listing opportunities, and what most potential buyers get completely wrong. In this chapter, I'll show you why your first job is to convince the seller you are absolutely the right buyer before you determine whether the company is the right fit for you.

Most inexperienced buyers will go into their first meeting with a seller without trusting them. They believe that the seller will want to convince them to buy the business regardless of whether or not it's a good fit for the buyer. They expect that the seller might be "unloading a business" before a change that will result in declining in value immediately following the purchase. They go in thinking that the seller is similar to a young entrepreneur trying to raise capital for a new venture. Buyers expect to be "pitched," and they want to know "the real reason" a seller is selling. Imagine if the banker quoted above was not interested in selling me on his bank. There would be little reason for me to care whether they got the loan or not. This is the exact approach most buyers take in meeting the seller.

Most buyers will go in aloof and reserved. They'll shoot down ideas and inject cautionary responses at opportune times. They act like a conservative investor who must be convinced to be brought to the table, and if they do, their actions warn, it's going to be hardball. This is not a *trust but verify* approach. It's a *prove it and then I'll consider trusting you* approach.

There is a time to be a conservative investor during this process. This book, however, is not about how to become a conservative investor; it's about acquisition entrepreneurship. Any acquisition will obviously include volumes of cautious investing analysis. Buying your first business is usually the largest investment you've ever made in your life and you will research accordingly. If there are snakes in the bushes, you will simply walk away later.

The best buyers, however, understand that they too are entrepreneurs, just like the seller. The transaction will be completed within a few months after meeting the seller and then the buyer will be in the driver's seat for the next four to forty years. Acting like an entrepreneur and not a venture capitalist during the interactions with the seller is the key to winning the seller over, getting the best deal outcome later, and behaving like the new CEO of the company—which you may or may not be, but that will be up to you and not them if you play your cards right.

Knowing that you and the seller will need to reach an agreement on deal terms down the road will likely require at least some level of negotiating. Understanding the seller's perspective and goals is the best way to build rapport and navigate the process ahead together toward the best outcome for all parties involved.

Let's take a walk in the seller's shoes.

Here's one seller profile: they've been running their business for years. Their spouse will tell you that they've lived and breathed their "baby," and there is little "spiritual" separation between the individual and the business—they are one and the same. Every employee that came and went, every customer issue, every good year was because of their initiatives, and every mistake made rested squarely on their shoulders. The company has provided income to their family, bought their house, and put their kids through private schools. For whatever reason, the timing is right to consider exiting the business.

Here's another: extremely skilled and building value from scratch, they started a project five years ago with the goal of building it to over $1 million in revenue. They put money, time, and sweat into building it and it's one of the biggest accomplishments of their life. They've hit their goal, and now, based on the original strategy, it's time to consider selling.

In both of these examples you can see that the business is a very intimate success story for the seller. This is not selling off a piece of equipment or a car. This is an *emotional* transaction for them.

After speaking with an M&A Advisor, they found out the market value of their company. It's significantly lower than they thought. They didn't understand what SDE was or what the multiples were for Main Street or lower middle-market companies. So, it took some time to digest and truly get ready to list the business for sale. They likely have taken measures over the last year or so to improve the marketability of the business. They want to make sure they get enough to retire—or at least maximize the value, because however much it is, it won't be enough. There's a lot at stake here. If you want to get emotional about anything, tie a large sum of money to it.

They're extremely concerned their customers, employees, or worse—their competition—will learn the company is for sale. They don't want to divulge anything they don't have to. After all, once a buyer comes to the table, they will need to determine whether they are dealing with a tire-kicker who will proactively look for reasons *not* to buy it or someone without the *means* to close.

They also have a reputation to uphold. Who is the new CEO of the company? Are they competent? Do they have a vision? Are they going to come in and terminate employees who have worked at the company for decades?

THE FIRST DATE

The best buyers understand that the fair price will reveal itself later, and if it doesn't, then you'll move on and find another one. In the meantime, your job is to convince the seller that you are the right buyer for the business because you are:

1. Able to close a deal if it's right, and not leave them "at the altar."

2. Competent in the management of, and can get passionate about, what is currently *their* company.

3. A trustworthy problem solver. Someone who can sit on the same side of the table as the seller and accomplish a *common* goal—to change ownership to you.

If you are able to convince the seller of these three things on the first call, you have already won. Let me show you how to accomplish all three of these in the first twenty minutes, and differentiate yourself from all other potential buyers.

WILLING AND ABLE TO CLOSE

Immediately building rapport with the listing broker and the seller will show them what you are not. Namely, an aloof conservative investor looking to get pitched their deal. Rather, you are good to work with, trustworthy, and able to keep your eyes on the objective—closing on a fair deal.

After evaluating an Offering Memorandum that catches your interest, you should reach out to the listing advisor and have a call with them. We've discussed previously what they'll be looking for, namely, someone who has the will and means to close a deal and is competent enough that they can present you to the seller. Consider this a screening interview.

Following that, typically, there will be the first seller meeting. If it's in the same geographic area, it will often start offsite, maybe at the broker's office, then move to the place of work, usually after employees have left for the day, or rescheduled for another time to visit when they are there.

COMPETENT AND PASSIONATE

The structure of the first meeting with the seller will start with opening comments by the advisor and will then typically turn to the buyer to give an introduction.

Relish this opportunity. This is the moment you paint the portrait of how easy it will be to work with you, how dedicated you are to closing if it's the right fit, and why you are the right candidate to take over.

Most potential buyers will give a short, passive description of their prior roles and maybe some accomplishments. They'll say nothing about the seller's business or what they, as buyers, are trying to accomplish. A good intermediary will pull this out during the conversation, but I encourage you to treat this first meeting like a job interview, where *you* are interviewing to be the CEO of the seller's company. Remember, having the right attitude is a critical component of the CEO mindset. It is here where it will start to move from theory to action.

Be respectful and polite. Thank them for taking the time to meet with you and let them know you are interested in their opportunity. Give a history of your background, highlighting relevant accomplishments. Explain why you're actively on the search, that you have a process, that you have taken the time to meet with banks and have arranged access to enough capital, and that you are committed to finding the right business in a certain timeframe. Compliment them by complimenting the business. Do this by highlighting a few characteristics that draw your interest to the company.

By doing this, you immediately comfort the seller. They can see that you like the business and therefore can get excited and passionate about it. They see that you acknowledge their hard work and success. They see that you are structured, prepared, and committed to buying the right company. Guess what just happened? Simply by approaching the buyer introduction as an interested entrepreneur ready to take the lead, you've approached the conversation the right way, and unlike the conservative investor who's expecting a deal pitch, you may have just become their favorite buyer.

I am not suggesting you be misleading, ingenuine, or manipulative. Only that I see this interview-style approach as the best way to get on the same side of the table as the seller and get them comfortable with you. This is the best way to build rapport. Keep in mind that most sellers will meet with a handful of potential buyers in the first few months. They're going on first dates with three to six people over the course of a few weeks with the goal of getting married a few months later. Who's going to win the bride?

COMMON GOAL

Shakespeare taught us that "all that glitters is not gold" and it's true here too, that even though the opportunity was attractive enough to have a meeting, it might not be of appropriate value to you personally. The odds of you meeting with more than one seller, or that a certain deal goes to another buyer, or doesn't check out in due diligence, is all part of the process. For whatever reason, you might not end up working with this particular seller, but nothing has been lost by approaching the seller as an enthusiastic entrepreneurial partner rather than a cynical angel investor. The deal will work out (or not), but establishing yourself early on as a partner and "good buyer" will also win you great favoritism with the intermediary. I have personally earned first looks on great opportunities many times over just from being a "good buyer." Reflecting back, I even acquired two of them.

Perhaps the short-term gain of this approach is that you immediately help the seller get comfortable with you. This is critical for many reasons, but the most of which is that the seller is the exact person who has *all the information* surrounding the business, and it's all confidential. You need as much confidential information as possible to properly assess a business opportunity. Getting the seller in a comfortable position to start sharing information, and working toward your goal by helping you get what you need in a timely manner later, is part of what you are hoping to accomplish. The first meeting should be all about the qualitative side of the business. Feel free to ask some softball financial clarification questions, but save the financial deep dive and hard questions for later. This is a first date. Like every first date the seller, and you, will highlight the strengths and downplay the weaknesses.

The criticism I get is that being polite, cooperative, and enthusiastic somehow puts you at a disadvantage when it comes to negotiations. As if being nice means that you leave all critical thinking at the door. I find this opinion is usually just influenced by outdated popular opinion, because all of the imperial evidence suggests otherwise. You can be nice but firm. Favoring a problem-solving partnership around a shared goal does not equate to automatic compromise or being taken advantage of.

Harvard published an article by Calum Coburn titled "Negotiation Conflict Styles"[68] that outlines five negotiation styles and when to use each. The article draws from the Lewicki and Hiam's Negotiation Matrix, which paints a portrait of different negotiating styles along axis representing varying degrees of cooperation and assertiveness (ranked from reactive to proactive).

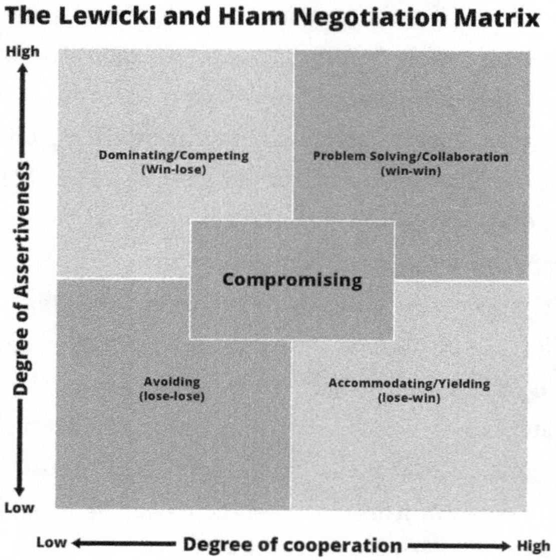

The Lewicki and Hiam Negotiation Matrix

Figure 8.1: The Lewicki and Hiam Negotiation Matrix[69]

---

68   https://hms.harvard.edu/sites/default/files/assets/Sites/Ombuds/files/Negotiation-ConflictStyles.pdf

69   Taken from http://purchasingpractice.com/developing-a-differentiated-negotiation-strategy/

An in-depth overview of when to use which strategy falls outside the scope of this book, but we do provide other resources on *BuyThenBuild.com* for you to further research your situation and the style that supports the best outcome. For now, be confident that should the time arise where you feel you need to avoid progress or can't agree on a particular component, you should leverage the intermediary. That is why they are there. They will prove incredibly valuable to keeping everyone on track toward the goal, especially when both sides feel they're at a standstill.

Research shows that a proactive, problem-solving, and cooperative approach toward a common goal results in the best outcomes for all parties, time and again. The common goal here, of course, is discovering the best possible deal for both sides. You are free to change your negotiation strategy at any time if you feel the situation has changed enough to support it. But remember, above all else, you don't have to acquire the business. If you feel like you're being lied to or taken advantage of (by the seller or the broker), I encourage you to run, not walk away.

Here's the other component of you negotiating strategy: negotiate everything you can, other than price, before you make a formal offer. Taking this approach allows you the discipline to identify what's important to the seller other than price. Is it future employment of key employees? Is it timing of the close? Is it not to hold a seller's note? Is it the ability to execute on one of their own growth strategies? Or is it just getting the highest price possible, no matter what?

Here's a clue: everyone says it's maximizing sale price, and while that's true, I have never seen a deal where the seller didn't have qualitative goals associated with their exit. Remember, this is a severely emotional and personal transaction with a lot at stake for the seller.

Identifying the deal points other than price will allow you to know where to focus your offer in order to give easy wins where you can. In fact, if the seller wants three specific things and it costs you nothing and you're willing to do them, do all of them. This comes at no cost to you, and you can pick your battles in the areas that are important to you. This is the win-win approach (we both get what we want) to the situation, as opposed to the win-lose (if you win, that means I have lost something). Figuring this out ahead of time will give you an edge in the nuances of the deal structure.

Let me give you an example. When selling my own company, there were two things critical to me for the transaction. First, the new CEO needed to have the skillset and means to take the company to the next level during industry transformation, and second, every single employee needed to be retained at the same (or fair market) pay rate.

The transaction value was important, sure, but I understood that would be determined based mostly on SDE and a multiple based on data—namely, comparative sales in our industry. If a buyer came in and didn't pass the first two requirements, there would be no deal.

Why was I selling? Actually, my business strategy was building new product lines internally and growing them aggressively through acquisition. We proactively contacted twenty-seven companies over two and a half years trying to find the right piece of the puzzle. Eventually, we found it and the potential seller shared my vision. It turned out he was more interested in buying than selling. By selling the company, I was able to achieve the vision I had for the future, albeit under different leadership.

DOWNLOADING THE SELLER'S BRAIN

Once you've established the right approach, it's time to dig into the business. This will likely take place over a couple of different meetings and will typically include a visit to the facility. While interviewing the seller, your objective is to determine the strengths and weaknesses of the business, the seller, and the industry. Between the numbers in the financial statements, the seller's story, and the industry research you execute, you are compiling the story behind the business: where it's been, where it's going, where it should be going, and what you bring to the table. So much of the benefit of this meeting will come from your ability to be an exceptional active listener.

Obviously, you are surveying for big concerns, such as industry decline, powerful competitors moving in, or customer concentration. The seller will not be telling you this directly, but they will often be telling you indirectly. It is your responsibility as the future CEO of this company to determine the strengths, weaknesses, opportunities, and threats surrounding the company. The seller is the best source of information; however, if there is something keeping them up at night, they likely won't bring it to the forefront on their own.

It is also your job to identify where the risks lie. Every business has risk associated with it. You as the buyer need to identify and either get comfortable with the risks involved (because they lie within in your skill set or are unlikely to occur) or determine the risks are too great and walk away.

Here are some tools and topics to guide you through the conversations with the seller.

SET THE TONE

Be optimistic around the opportunity but tremendously concerned about the risks involved. This will allow you to see the opportunity as it is. Most tire-kickers spend the entire first meeting identifying why the business is a bad investment rather than identifying the opportunity as a whole. Where are the opportunities and where are the risks of this business? What would need to be true for you to grow this company to double its size? These are the questions you are asking yourself.

Keep in mind that you are not leaving your critical thinking skills at the door. The seller will have their answers, but be aware they are probably not going to give you the entire answer, warts and all. Why would they? It's their life's work, it's confidential information, they just met you, and yes, you might buy it, so they want to present it well. So take it all at face value, leverage them for their knowledge and insight, get a feel for who they are as a person, and all the while, simply try to identify where the risks and opportunities are.

SMOKE SCREENS

One way that has helped me do this is by asking the same question a few different ways at various points in the meeting (and repeatedly in future meetings with the seller). In doing so, I am usually able to pick up new information and round out a more complete, three-dimensional answer.

In the same regard, people typically have a planned response for questions they want to avoid, so if you get the same, canned answer every time, you can figure out where you're getting a smoke screen. By making notes to drill down at a future meeting, you can identify the areas you want to get comfortable with before buying the company. Identifying the "rabbit holes" in the story and the numbers will be the areas you'll really get into during due diligence. For now, at the beginning, you are more identifying these areas for homework and follow up, rather than trying to answer every big strategic question.

ELEMENT OF SURPRISE

I also like to move around a lot in my line of questioning. I find this throws off momentum around a certain topic. If the conversation starts leaning toward customer concentration in a specific geographical area, for example, they might be anticipating the next question will be around why that is. Ask it later and instead inquire about how the company is positioned within the industry or how much inventory they keep on hand. Then double back with your question around customer concentration. I find by progressing with a few different lines of questions simultaneously you can get the most honest answers because it throws off the logic behind what's going to come next. Most people are always thinking about what they're going to say next, so when you switch topics, it can result in more raw answers, which may help you build a more accurate company portrait.

You'll need to determine what, exactly, is going to walk out the door with the seller. Do your best to determine where the seller's personal skillset lies and what customer relationships they have. Determine how *transferrable* the business is.

SELLER STRENGTHS

People tend to put energy into the activities where they excel, and the core competency of the business is usually directly related to the seller's area of expertise. If the seller is an operations person, generally you don't need to worry about the customers leaving because the processes necessary to endure will be in place. On the other hand, if the seller is the lead salesperson, you'll know that you need to direct your immediate attention to nurturing customer relationships. Whatever the seller's skillset may be, it is an area of the business that will need direct and swift attention by you.

OVERVIEW: GENESIS AND EVOLUTION

I always initiate a seller interview with, "Tell me about your business." This question invariably leads to the entire history of the company, the "genesis" story, and how it got to where it is now. While the seller recounts the birth and growth of the business, listen to see if they articulate the value proposition. Even if they do, wait for them to finish and follow up with, "What makes this company different?" or "Why do people buy from you?"

You likely received a customer breakout in the OM and noted any customer concentration concerns. If there is a particularly large customer, ask why they, specifically, buy from the company.[70] The best answer is related to the value proposition of the company; the second best is they have a long-term relationship with someone who will remain after the seller leaves. The most challenging answer is, "I play golf with the owner," or, "We've been going to the same church for twenty years." Then this gives you insight into how the company currently sells its products to its largest customers. The question for you becomes, "Can that style be replicated by me?" or, "How does it scale?" There may or may not be a good answer for this, but there is a right one.

---

70 Note, however, that the seller interview and the OM are not appropriate times to be asking for the names of the specific customers. This is the seller's confidential information and should be revealed only after an offer has been accepted.

Typically, the seller's story will highlight the areas to dig deeper. Don't interrupt, listen closely, and let them tell you where to go with the conversation.

They likely covered their background, but if they didn't, get their story. What are their areas of interest and skillsets? What do they do inside the business? What does their day to day look like? If it's a small company, you'll want to ask if their spouse also works in the business (if so, you'll have to absorb both of their tasks).

Even understanding how much vacation they take will tell you how married or essential the owner is in day-to-day operations. Some owners take two weeks every quarter, while others haven't been on a vacation in ten years. This is also part of the "bus test": if the owner got hit by a bus, what would happen to the business?

CUSTOMER MAKE UP

Get a sense of what revenue comes from which product, and then, try to tack a gross profit to the response. Oftentimes, the owner will bundle complimentary services or products around their core offerings, and that is information you need to know about in advance of purchase. This can add insight to the financial analysis you've already done. What you are looking for is which products add to revenue, which add to gross margin, and are they the same?

Who is the customer? Are there different customer segments? Where do they live, how old are they, and what is their motivation to buy in the first place? Is it a pain they are getting a solution to? Is it a required, unemotional purchase? What percentage is repeat business versus new? How do the customers find the company?

COMPETITION

Who are the competitors? What would the competitors say they did better than this company? What makes this company different? What is the best way to learn more about the industry?

GROWTH OPPORTUNITIES

What is the path to growth? Why do they believe this is the single best path? Have they had success doing an activity that scales or is it a new initiative? Why have they not executed it themselves? Often, the seller's perspective of future opportunity is rooted in a problem or an obstacle that needs to be addressed—either in the company or the industry.

CHALLENGES AND THREATS

What is the biggest challenge facing the business? What is the biggest threat facing the business? What would need to happen for the company to cease to exist?

DRIVER FOR EXIT

Why are you selling? I never ask this question up front. It is the most anticipated question by the seller and the broker and they have an answer before the company is listed. I find that if I ask it up front, I get the same answer as the OM and the same answer as the broker told me in the screening call. If you ask it after you have built rapport, presented yourself well, listened to their story, and understand the business better, you may be able to put pieces together. Your follow-up questions will be more insightful, and you may begin to understand the real answer a little better.

There are some answers buyers absolutely love. Death or illness, sometimes divorce, and the seventy-eight-year-old simply wanting to retire. These are all horrible circumstances for the seller, but the truth is typically evident in these situations. Oddly, I even put sellers looking for a liquidity event into this category. If they've started a business, grown it for three to five years, and are looking to sell what they've built, it's pretty straightforward and a common practice. The entire venture capital and private equity industries are based on this exact principle. It is bleeding over into entrepreneurship healthily and is another reason why acquisition entrepreneurship can be such a rewarding avenue. Some of the best acquisitions can come from somebody just wanting to take some chips off the table.

Other answers, such as they're burnt out or bored, looking at a new opportunity, or relocation, aren't as evident as the real answer. You'll want to spend more time exploring here to see what you can learn. If you can't find a compelling reason for someone to walk away from a cash cow, trust me, there is a reason, and it likely hasn't reared its ugly head yet.

Is the business tanking? Have they lost market share? Have sales flatlined? If the seller is bored, chances are all of the employees are bored too. Figure out where the company is in the lifecycle of the industry—is this a tremendous opportunity or an offering circling the drain of obsolescence?

IDEAL BUYER PROFILE

What does the ideal purchaser look like? Get a sense for the skillset required. It will likely look like the skillset needed for the growth plan; after all, this is the logical addition to the company. That said, try to understand whether it's realistic that the next owner take over the duties of the current CEO as well as the new duties.

INDUSTRY TRENDS

What are the best sources for additional industry information and trends? Is the seller willing to stay on with the business after the sale, and if so, for how long?

PERSONNEL

Who are the key people in the company? If they were buying it, what changes would they make? Who is critical, and who is not performing?

THE IMMEDIATE FUTURE

Find out what they plan to do after the sale and what their future looks like. This can reveal a lot about them and where they are emotionally with the decision to sell. Toward the end of the initial meeting, expand on new information that came out during the conversation and address any lingering concerns you still have.

CULTURE

A friend of mine was looking for, and ultimately acquired, a product distribution company. He found during the process of meeting and working with the seller that that he didn't really care for him at all. After the closing, he discovered that the unfavorable personality traits of the seller were well established in the culture of the company and some of the seller's explanations were inaccurate, probably by design. He clashed with the majority of employees from day one and had to fight an uphill battle to win them over. He wound up losing most of the key managers and it took years for him to right the ship and get the team in harmony. He spent the first few years cycling through personnel. Which is fine, in that acquisition entrepreneurs are built to do whatever it takes. But this activity greatly detracts from the benefits of acquisition entrepreneurship in the first place. It is important that you listen to your intuition while working with the seller. You don't have to be best friends, but with the exception of a turnaround opportunity, sharing the same values as the seller will reflect greatly on the business you are considering. After meeting the seller and getting a feel for this, the best way to support your impression is to get a tour of the business.

Getting a tour of the business can tell you multitudes about the culture and flavor. Cleanliness, orderliness, focused or unfocused employees, new or outdated assets. These will all be exposed during a tour. Can you pick up on the CEO's relationship with their employees? Is it healthy or unhealthy? Is there a sense of urgency, or does it have a relaxed tone? Remember, the seller will likely be on edge, not wanting the employees to suspect anything. If you are introduced, you'll likely be introduced as some kind of consultant or prospective customer.

Ask questions about how things work and flow through the building—get details. Are the employees encouraged to interact with you? Take it all in and apply it to your story of the business, which should be coming together for you.

Culture is probably the single most overlooked aspect of a potential target company by buyers, yet it's a critical piece of the puzzle and essential to understanding your plan for how to manage the company from day one.

John Bly, author of *Cracking the Code*, is a CPA and acquisition entrepreneur, having grown his firm through several acquisitions. After several decades of practice, he's become an expert in acquiring businesses. The very first thing he does when considering a new acquisition is go out to lunch with the seller. If they don't have a connection or establish a rapport in the first meeting, Bly doesn't go any further with the deal. He knows how vital a company's culture is to its success, and he knows it comes directly from the top down. This might be significantly more critical when growing through acquisition as opposed to acquiring a platform company to launch from, but no matter how you slice it, culture is a critical element to success.

SELLER AFTER CLOSING

It's interesting how every time I acquire a company I want to make sure the seller is committed to a long transition period. This, of course, is critical so that you can get all the information possible to be successful learning the ins and outs of the new business.

That said, a few fundamental things happen immediately after the closing.

First, all of the employees understand that they now work for the new owner, you, not the seller. As a result, they will align themselves with the new owner immediately. It's amazing how fast this can happen. But in a way, it's their first day on the job. There is no transition period in the employee's eyes, the customer's eyes, or as you'll find out, the seller's eyes—it's immediate. There will be some "playing both sides of the field" going on, but it will pass when the seller departs the business.

Second, the seller, with the deal closed and money in the bank, is spiritually, physically, and mentally ready to leave as soon as possible. They are financially unattached to the business for the first time in years, and just as the employees want to get to know their new source of income (you, the new CEO), the seller is aggressively looking toward the next thing as well. Even with a seller note or earnout in place, the lion's share of the transaction has likely already occurred, their attention is elsewhere, and their role will rapidly dissolve into a purposeless existence.

Third, what you'll learn from the seller at this point is the minutia. It's important. It's critical. But it's also task-oriented, execution stuff. These are not the tasks of a business that make it hard to run; these are the easy, day-to-day action items. You will learn these in the first two days. Though it may be only 80 percent at first, you'll truly be done with the seller other than some quick phone calls throughout the first thirty days. You'll also transition over the supplier accounts to your name or your entity, which will occur in the first eight hours.

Fourth, you will understand that you really don't need them around and that you won't want them around. You will not have full control while they are there. You may find you even have a lot of questions during the first few weeks, or even month, but you will very likely not need them for day to day information after the first month is over.

So, although you'll likely want to negotiate owner's involvement following closing, my position typically goes like this: get them out as soon as you can (but not a moment earlier). Following the first couple of days, it's better to have many short interactions, rather than keep them around.

The seller will be critical during the acquisition process and the first month after closing, but usually not much after. Their emotional connection is gone. I'm sharing this early because it's a natural part of the seller's journey, and the more times you see it, the more you'll know it's coming when you enter into a new acquisition agreement. Understanding that the seller's connection with the business is both financial and personal offers insight to how emotional the journey can be for them and how little motivation they will have to stick around after closing.

FIRST MEETING REFLECTION

Following the first meeting, you will have learned a lot about the business. You'll have the story and insight into the financials and performance; you'll be familiar with the product of service, and you'll have a feel for the culture. You will have a deeper insight into the company than many of the employees ever will.

Spend some time immediately following the meeting reflecting on the business. Does it fit your target statement? Can you get excited about the business? Will you take pride in being the CEO of this company? What did you like and dislike about the company? What is the biggest threat facing the company? What is the single greatest opportunity for the business, and does it match your skillset?

It's critical you stay goal-oriented at this point. Here's why: most potential buyers never get past this step. They look and they "shop" but they never close a deal. Why? What are they looking for?

In my experience, they followed the wrong "process" from the beginning. They didn't commit to buy in a certain time frame; they didn't spend time understanding the Three As, they didn't evaluate their skillsets; they didn't consider what they want their day to day to look like; they measured size in revenue and not SDE; they didn't understand that opportunity profiles can be very different, much less identify which one they are actually looking for.

Instead, they focused on industry. They worked without deadlines or a sense of urgency. These potential buyers certainly didn't create a target statement. As a result, these would-be buyers will be stuck. They will attempt to weigh all the variables *after* they have gotten this far in the process. This is a recipe to never accomplish their acquisition entrepreneurship goals. They simply don't know what they are looking for—even if they are physically standing inside the business.

Obviously, this is not permission to be hasty, but it is important to underscore that you have already done all the preparation ordinary potential buyers didn't. You know at this point, with clarity, whether the business is a good potential fit for you. You are not the ordinary potential buyer—you are the acquisition entrepreneur who completed the extra work to get ready. In the words of two-time Super Bowl winning head coach Jimmy Johnson, "The difference between ordinary and extraordinary is that little extra." Congratulate yourself, you are the elite athlete of potential buyers.

During your immediate reflection on the meeting, ask yourself this question: What would need to be true for you to make an offer to acquire this company?

This question will help you build a roadmap for the next steps. Either you pass on this opportunity (and keep looking), you write an offer, or you define real next steps for yourself. By identifying what's standing in your way to making an offer, you are identifying where your search needs to go next. What information do you need that you don't have?

If you sense that you might make an offer on this company, you'll already be thinking about the structure of the deal you'd like to see. However, even if you are ready to make an offer, you need to take the time to back up, review the industry, and begin to put a business plan together. You have just spent time zoomed in on the individual business without insight on the ocean it's swimming in.

I believe in taking calculated risks, but it's essential to start outlining the benefit-to-risk ratio, and where you believe you can take this company. The best way to do this is not by looking at the company itself and deciding on a gut feeling, it's by understanding the industry trends at large and seeing what's happening and what is possible. Applying business strategy frameworks and various growth models to quantifiable information about the industry will help you determine and project the plan forward for this company. This is precisely the subject of the next chapter.

CHAPTER 9

DESIGNING THE FUTURE

THE DREAM OF ACQUISITION ENTREPRENEURS IS TO BUILD value in their own company. The challenge is to find an acquisition, build a plan, then execute that plan. This chapter offers helpful frameworks you'll need to evaluate the target acquisition and build your plan.

Once you have identified a company you are interested in acquiring, you need to take time to understand the industry as a whole and the specific company's position in that industry. I offer two effective frameworks to guide your research and will walk you through the different levels of business strategy.

From there, you will need to develop a business plan. We'll look at a way to determine the driver of the business and some tools to help you create an effective business plan quickly.

Last, I want you to dream. By considering a few existing frameworks that have resulted in explosive growth and exponential value creation in both startups and existing businesses, you'll have the ability to see the bold visions that can act as a north star to the best opportunities in your new acquisition, and the ambitious goals that come as a result.

UNDERSTANDING THE INDUSTRY AND THE BUSINESS MODEL

Contrary to popular belief, most businesses in the world don't have a significantly unique offering. Instead, it's more common to rely on *differences* from competitors. These sometime fall in areas like market positioning, marketing channels, key relationships, equipment, or geography. Knowing what makes a company different is more important, especially in mature markets, than what makes it better.

Understanding the business model will help outline the existing strengths, threats, and trends within an industry and a business. We'll look at Porter's Five Forces and the Lifecycle of Industry as tools for highlighting the economics of an industry and the differences that exist in a specific company as a result.

PORTER'S FIVE FORCES

Michael Porter is a revered economist and corporate strategist from Harvard University who literally wrote the books on *Competitive Strategy* and *Competitive Advantage*. He first introduced his Five Forces model in *Harvard Business Review* in 1979.[71] Today, they represent a cornerstone of corporate strategy education in business schools and board rooms across the globe.

Porter's Five Forces provide a framework for identifying where the power lies in the supply chain, where the threats exist in an existing business model, and where the strengths of a company's value proposition can be found.

By considering the overall industry, and then a specific business, as it applies to each force, you can begin to understand the state of the industry and the position of the company within that industry.

---

71   Michael Porter, "How Competitive Forces Shape Strategy," *Harvard Business Review*, 1979.

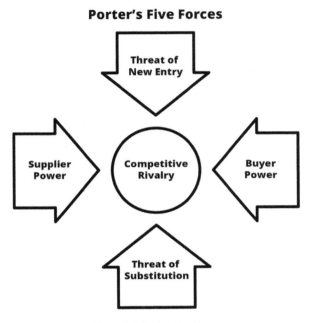

Figure 9.1: Porter's Five Forces

THE THREAT OF NEW ENTRANTS

The threat of new entrants refers directly to Warren Buffet's concept of the "moat." In other words, does the company provide something that allows it to fend off new companies from entering the market and taking existing market share? Buffet's long-used example of the ideal business being the only toll road across a river might apply as a good analogy here. Spend time identifying the barriers to entry that exist. If someone else wanted to start a similar business, what would keep them out?

The threat of new entrants is typically kept at bay with competitive tools such as differentiation, brand equity, economies of scale, switching costs, cost of starting up, access to distribution channels, geographic restrictions, or the new favorite, network effects. Does the target business hold any protection from this threat? How strong is it?

THE THREAT OF SUBSTITUTES

The threat of substitutes refers to analyzing the value the product or service has to the customer. Is there a potential easier way to accomplish the same or similar goal for the customer? This points not to direct competition over the same product, but rather to understanding the value being received by the customer and identifying what else may provide that benefit. It's easy to think about new technologies moving in and eating market share, such as cell phones overtaking landlines or tablets eating away at laptops. I try to consider the offering at the highest level; for example, television and books both provide home entertainment, so understanding the trend surrounding substitutes at this level could prove insightful, and perhaps enough to develop a strategy around diversification, if it made sense.

BUYER POWER

Consider the power customers have to drive prices down. This will show you how much "buyer power" exists in an industry. If there are a few large buyers and many fragmented suppliers, this gives particular strength to the buyers to put suppliers in direct competition against each other in a race to the lowest price. This concept is typically thought of as *commoditization*. The industry might be ripe for either a disruptive technology or consolidation play—either of which could be executed by an acquisition entrepreneur with the right plan.

SUPPLIER POWER

Supplier power is the opposite of buyer power. It speaks to how easy it is for the company's suppliers to increase prices, which in turn increases cost of goods sold and reduces gross margins. How many suppliers are there? How unique is their product? How difficult is it to switch? Or, in today's world, could the supplier cut out the target business altogether and sell directly to buyers online? How strong is the distribution channel?

COMPETITION

Industry rivalry is likely the core of where your research will be for this phase. Understanding who the competitors are, how competitive the market is, the position of each of the competing entities, and what their value proposition is will lead you to an understanding of all the players. Look for quantifiable data showing trends in the industry. Get industry reports and comparable company financials if you can. This will help you understand the performance in the industry as well as help identify new opportunities or differentiators.

APPLYING THE FORCES

As you apply Porter's Five Forces to the acquisition target and its industry, a picture will emerge that will provide the foundation for how attractive the business is in its current state. As you review, ask yourself what new management could do to leverage or change any threats or opportunities.

In the same regard, acquiring a business has inherent risk. By applying the forces, you should be able to clearly identify what the risks are with a specific business and whether you are comfortable with the level of risk or not.

Another key component that will help understand the state of the industry is where it is in the lifecycle.

THE LIFECYCLE OF INDUSTRY

Everything has a lifecycle. Every year has four seasons; humanity has childhood, adolescence, adulthood, and old age; and every industry experiences introduction, growth, maturity, and decline. In addition to Porter's Five Forces, I continually apply knowledge of the lifecycle of industry to a particular opportunity and attempt to gauge where they are, right at the beginning of analysis. This can help frame the proper strategy to employ in a given opportunity.

At the beginning of every industry, a new product or service has a birth. Perhaps this is through the vehicle of invention, or deregulation, or a new way of being able to deliver an existing solution. Regardless, industries in the introduction phase tend to have low revenue and high expenses. The future demand for the product is often in question as the market is literally being created.

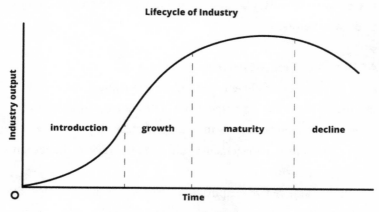

Figure 9.2: Lifecycle of Industry

The introduction phase of an industry is when the offering, or value proposition, is still being worked out. Potential customers of the product do not even know the product exists in the first place, and if they do, they may not completely understand the value of the new offering. Often, quality levels are too low to make a meaningful impact on a marketplace. This is a critical time for customer feedback loops and capital funding. The uniqueness of the offering is highlighted and is typically embraced by what author Geoffrey Moore coined "early adopters." Like an infant, the fragile industry has sparkling potential in its eye, but it requires a lot of love and attention.

If the industry moves beyond the introduction phase, it moves into the growth phase. This is when customers begin to understand that the offering exists and the value it provides. Demand grows significantly. This is the adolescent or growth phase.

Consider the number of internet users in the United States from 1997 to 2007. According to research at the World Bank and Statistica, in 1997 there were under 60 million internet users, or about 21.6 percent of the country—already a significant portion of the population considering a new technology—but just three years later the number of users doubled. Seven years after that, it had doubled again to 226 million, or about 75 percent of the US population. This is an example of tremendous growth during a short period.

Adolescent markets are the arena of venture capital-backed startups. This is the time that invents heroes and huge buyouts. VC firms are made famous by good plays during this time and startups that can manage the execution risk and succeed in getting big.

Growth is followed by maturity, a time when an industry shakeout rids unprofitable, low quality, or unfocused players. Consolidation and bankruptcies take their toll as market demand levels off and the players begin to actually have to compete with each other for the first time.

Eternally profitable companies are found in mature industries. These companies are no longer "sexy," their technology is no longer new, and you won't find their CEOs on the covers of magazines—but they make up the bulk of the economy. Perhaps this is also why search funds tend to look for companies holding a sustainable position in fragmented industries.[72]

Often consolidation strategies emerge in mature industries as well. Fragmented, slow-growth markets provide opportunities through connecting multiple locations into one company. Additional acquisitions tend to be even more affordable than the first one, and growth through acquisition can be very aggressive. One company generating $8 million in revenue acquiring another company generating $8 million in revenue is very affordable in mature industries where valuation multiples are significantly lower than growth industries and provide a source of aggressive growth by any measure.

The best examples of the immense opportunity surrounding mature industries are the high-growth companies within them. *Gazelles,* or companies that experience 20 percent or more top line growth for a period of four years or more tend to be in established industries that happen to be trending the right direction at that time.

You need look no further than the highly coveted *Inc.* 500 awards and the companies that win them. Last year, the five largest industries represented in the *Inc.* 500 were healthcare, business-to-business products and services, financial services, IT services, and construction. None of these are adolescent markets. It just takes an effective approach in a mature market to build exceptional companies.

---

72   *https://www.forbes.com/sites/vanessaloder/2014/08/07/the-search-fund-model-how-to-become-a-twenty-six-year-old-ceo-if-youre-willing-to-kiss-frogs/#1b52781b1190*

Often, "innovation" can come inexpensively. Imagine if Blockbuster had used their DVD library, a website, and the US mail to allow consumers to request and return rentals? We may not even know what Netflix is today.[73] All the pieces were there—it's just about connecting the right dots. DVD rental was not a growth industry at the time. On the contrary, it was a mature industry in consolidation mode. Further, there is nothing particularly disruptive about a DVD, a website, and the US Postal Service—all the tools used by Netflix to take down an industry giant.

The period of all of these lifecycle phases is dependent on the industry itself and how long-term an offering might be. A company in a growth industry, for example, might be having good times today, only to experience technological innovation that makes it obsolete in a number of months, while other industries experience decades of comfortable adulthood. The acquisition entrepreneur needs to consider all aspects of an industry to identify the opportunity.

Consider the book printing industry. Book printing has been around since Guttenberg, and yet the 1990s was the strongest decade in human history for book printing. This was followed in the late 2000s with bookstores going out of business, the invention of the Kindle and iPad, the first strong emergence of electronic alternatives, and online ordering of digitally manufactured, print-on-demand titles.

Acquisition entrepreneurs see the opportunity at any industry stage but tend to lend themselves to more mature industry companies with solid upside opportunity if executed effectively. Knowing

---

73 I owe credit to Washington University's Olin School of Business Assistant Dean and Director of Executive Education, Samuel Chun, for bringing to my attention that the core "disruptive technologies" used by Netflix was to use envelopes, DVDs, and the US Postal Service. His presentation on the topic is nothing short of remarkable.

where the current company fits in the lifecycle is often the first step to identifying what types of opportunities exists for the company.

Applying Porter's Five Forces and the Opportunity Profile Matrix from Chapter 4, can help identify the opportunities and threats an organization has. This is often enough to set a fundamental understanding of the best and worst the company has to offer you as the acquisition entrepreneur.

MARKET RESEARCH

It's critical to your understanding that you conduct as much market research as possible. Understanding the industry and the market will help you firmly identify the driver of the business, the strengths and weaknesses of the business and the industry, who the customers are, and perhaps most importantly, the underlying trends.

As you move forward with industry research and begin to apply the frameworks discussed in this chapter, write down the strengths and weakness of the company in a similar way you did for yourself during the Law of Three As analysis you did in the preparation phase. After all, this is the match you are trying to make—you to your company.

Then, identify the trends in the industry. Look for industry data and research to actually quantify the trend. The empirical evidence will typically suggest what the future of the industry looks like. It will also highlight where the best opportunities lie for any specific company in that industry that can capitalize on the trend. I take the approach that there is a right answer to every question, and the identification of the best business strategy often lies in identifying what the empirical evidence suggests doing. In other words, the foundation of the company is in what it is presently doing, but the future may require pivoting the mission to include where the industry is going.

Strengths, weaknesses, and trends can outline what is the single best opportunity for the company and what is currently holding them back. Often, trends today are vastly different from when the company started. The core competency, or special sauce, might need an upgrade to tackle a new opportunity in the industry.

We've reviewed the fact that buyers want to know why the seller is selling. They are fearful that there might be a significant change to the business just on the horizon, either an industry-wide transformation or something specifically impacting the business, geography, competitor—something. But please understand this: the owner of every business, including the seller, has encountered and dealt with business challenges. You will too. They didn't always know what was on the horizon. Neither will you.

It is true that they might know something they don't want to share. It is common for someone about to go out of business to try to list the company for sale. These are all true. But most companies for sale are not trying to sell because they are about to go out of business. Just try to figure out what the current challenges could be.

One thing is for sure: you will be facing a business challenge as the CEO of the company. Either in the near future or the medium future. Solving problems is the day-to-day activity of the CEO. The more you can predict what that challenge will be, before buying the company, the better. Running through Porter's Five Forces, the industry lifecycle, and underlying trends will help give you a sense of where to look for this future challenge.

The internet is clearly the best vehicle for conducting industry research today, and throughout the book we've highlighted other tools such as IBIS, Statistica, and the BRG (Business Reference Guide). These are all paid options, but there is an abundance of information you can learn by contacting industry associations.

BUSINESS STRATEGY

Business strategy can help you frame the right questions and understand the value drivers of a specific business. For example, why is the company in business? What is its core competency? What customer market is served? What value do they receive? What customers should continue to be served? Which ones should it start serving? Which products or services are offered or should be offered? What makes us different than the competition? Should we grow? Should there be new products developed? New territories?

Outlining your research objectives by addressing the different levels of business strategy will help you think through each level of the business clearly. These will guide you through which questions to ask when and will guide your thinking and decision making.

There are three levels of business strategy: corporate, competitive, and growth.

CORPORATE STRATEGY

Corporate strategy is the highest level of consideration. This is the mission, vision, and values of the organization. This is the identification of what you want to accomplish with the business and what your goals are as the CEO. In almost every instance, identifying why the business exists in the first place is more important than what makes it different. Clearly, you are excited about the business and what it can become. What business is it in? This is where that vision and mission are outlined.

COMPETITIVE STRATEGY

Competitive strategy identifies the best offering to accomplish the company's vision. Competitive strategy applies the core competencies of the business to specific markets. Said another way, it highlights who the customer is and why they would buy from the company. It outlines how the company will sustain a competitive advantage, typically through investment, innovation, or productivity improvements. It speaks to the pain being addressed by the offering or the luxury being experienced by the customer. This is where the strengths, weaknesses, and trends from your research will be applied. What is the pain being addressed? What is the "special sauce"?

GROWTH OR MARKET STRATEGY

Market strategy outlines the path to growth. Often, market strategy will address the desire to increase market share, even at the expense of short term earnings. (Think Amazon.) Growth strategy typically pulls from one (or many) of four broad plays: diversification, product development, market penetration, and market development. This is the "how we plan to sell more stuff" part.

WHAT DRIVES VALUE?

What is the one thing that drives revenue? If there was one metric that could measure the overall performance of the company, what would it be? How can you accelerate or multiply what drives revenue? Understanding what would need to be true in order to double the size of the business is typically a derivative of understanding this metric.

One of the best books ever written on business is Jim Collins' *Good to Great: Why Some Companies Make the Leap and Others Don't*. In it, Collins reports the results of the most in-depth research likely ever done around high performing companies. One common denominator among the sustained, best-performing public companies in history is what Collins calls the "hedgehog concept." This concept points to an organization's ability to continually make decisions based on an underlying, crystal-clear understanding of the intersection of three areas, and achieve superior economic returns as a result. Those areas are: (1) what you are deeply passionate about, (2) what you can be the best in the world at, and (3) what best drives your economic engine.

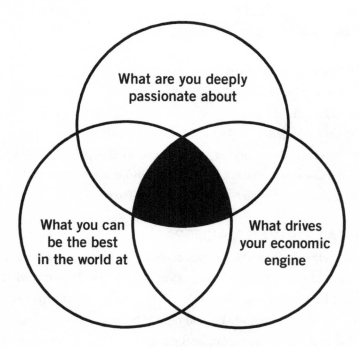

Figure 9.3 Jim Collins' Hedgehog Concept

When you identify the intersection of those three areas, you are able to build sustaining momentum around your vision for the company. Collins even suggests that living by the *Good to Great* principles, managers are able to get world-class results, even in mature or declining industries. "You absolutely do not need to be in a great industry to produce sustained great results. No matter how bad the industry, every good-to-great company figured out how to produce truly superior economic returns." There is more to the great companies that Collins profiles in his book, but the hedgehog concept is the first step to creating such a culture. In turn, this concept is such a powerful tool for acquisition entrepreneurs in analyzing and deciding on how to move forward before purchasing a business. Creating a vision and a strategy for your company grounded in this concept can have you prepared among the best.

Thinking through and applying the Hedgehog Concept to an acquisition target will bring clarity to the single activity which drives value throughout the organization and to its customers.

DEVELOPING A BUSINESS PLAN

As the strengths, weaknesses, trends, and drivers come together, the specific opportunity the acquisition target provides will come into focus. It's time to develop your business plan.

Sure, the bank will want to review this plan, but more importantly, the exercise will help you engineer the future of the company you want to acquire. Further, the exercise will get you organized, set a vision, and take a big step toward designing the future of the company you will buy then build.

The problem with formal business plans is that they can be hundreds of pages, overly academic, and complicated to implement because of the sheer size of them. Personally, I consider this a wasted effort. Much of what comes out of that process is gleamed simply from outlining your thoughts and getting it in front of people who would consider investing or lending you the capital to execute. This is better executed with a short executive summary and a pitch deck.

VC investor and author Guy Kawasaki wrote a blog post titled, "The Only 10 Slides You Need in a Pitch," echoing the philosophies

from his book, *The Art of the Start*. The deck is intended for startup
companies to address only the biggest questions and get to the meat
of each issue quickly. Every time I am developing a startup idea or
acquisition I create slides from this template, then create a written
Executive Summary from the results. You can find a link to the post
on *BuyThenBuild.com*, but we'll review the concepts here.

TITLE

Name and location of the business, slogan, and contact information.

PROBLEM

Every business should be solving "a pain." What is the problem the
business is addressing? Or is it providing a luxury? Clearly identify
the pain or opportunity, as well as who it's for.

VALUE PROPOSITION

What is the company's solution to the problem? What is the offering and unique competitive advantage of the company in supplying
this offering?

UNDERLYING MAGIC

What's the "secret sauce" of the company? What do they have that
the competition doesn't? Is there "a moat"? What is the core competency? Is there an advantage in technology, IP, brand, geography,
or other area?

BUSINESS MODEL

Here, I like to run through a business model canvas. It's a separate
exercise that will help you map, design, and assess the model of the
business. You can find a link to a downloadable copy at *BuyThen-
Build.com*.

GO-TO-MARKET PLAN

Remember that revenue driver? How do you plan to continue running a profitable business, how do you plan to grow the business, and why will it flourish under your leadership?

COMPETITIVE ANALYSIS

Provide a complete view of the competitive landscape. How competitive is the industry? The exercise of putting together a perception map is worthwhile here. Under what two axes would you define the industry? How would you define the position of your target company in this? This is much more difficult in a mature market than a startup, but working through the exercise will help you think about how the industry is defined and the company's position within that industry.

MANAGEMENT TEAM

Highlight what you (and your partner or partners, if you have them) bring to the table. What is your background and experience, and why you are right for the job?

FINANCIAL PROJECTIONS AND KEY METRICS

When acquiring a company, you'll want to project out three years into the future. How much will the company grow? Will you maintain gross margin percentage? Will your expenses increase? Is growth slow and steady?

CURRENT STATUS, TIMELINE, SOURCES, AND USES OF FUNDS

Where is the deal? Do you have a signed Letter of Intent? When do you expect to take ownership? Do you require funding for just the company or do you need inventory, working capital, or real estate?

Can you see how Kawasaki's slides cover everything we outlined in corporate, competitive, and market level strategy? It's extremely effective in helping you outline your plan and communicate it quickly and effectively.

FORECASTING

Once you have a solid grasp on the financial history of the company and have examined the trends, put together a complete forecast for the next three years. You can find additional guidance on how to outline this on *BuyThenBuild.com*.

The exercise of looking forward is extremely useful in getting a handle on what you are trying to do with the business. If revenue has been growing, is it likely to continue growing? What impact can you have on sales, management, cost of goods, staffing, and other overall improvements? Ask yourself both general and specific questions. Growth costs money. How will you pay for it? Will the expense come all at once or in phases? Most small businesses lack sophisticated IT systems and marketing programs. Are these areas you intend to invest in? Going through each line of the financial statements and projecting out the impact on each line will help you understand the current and future of your company.

An acquisition entrepreneur may have different growth strategies for the business than the current owner. How much extra cash will you need to allocate to growth strategies and initial improvements? What is the estimated purchase price for the business and how much debt will you take on? How is the debt going to affect the total profitability of the company? Will you have to increase operating expenses to build additional infrastructure for growth and marketing new products? Bear in mind, interest payments can be taken out pre-tax, but the principal payments are post-tax. Do you have outside equity investors or will there be seller financing? These are all factors that contribute to your calculations. Take it from the top and work your way through all of the costs, expenses, and variables.

You'll find there will be three stages of financial analysis as you go through the process of acquisition: "back of the napkin" projections are fine at the initial Offering Memorandum review. As you prepare to write a Letter of Intent to purchase, you'll want to get more specific in your mind about how this will look in the future. Finally, after a Letter of Intent is agreed upon, you'll need to firm up your business plan and financial projections.

FRAMEWORKS FOR EXPLOSIVE GROWTH

Robert Slee, author of *Time Really is Money* and *Private Capital Markets*, proclaimed that almost all small and medium-sized businesses don't provide value over and above the cost of the capital invested in their companies. In short, the businesses you're looking at are actually providing negative value to the economy. If you agree with Slee's conclusion, the opportunity to take the platform and create value through innovation, operational creativity, or market segment differentiation provides a landscape of tremendous potential for those willing to walk the path. The inventory of available companies needs the entrepreneur as much as the entrepreneur needs it.

An acquisition entrepreneur has the advantage of bringing a greater vision to transform the existing company into something of even greater value. There are so many business books out there with tremendous, game-changing ideas. Applying these models to acquisition entrepreneurship can reveal new opportunities for existing companies. By looking at some of these, you may be able to apply changes in existing companies that can result in substantial or even exponential growth.

I want to highlight a few of these ideas that can help you think about taking your acquisition target to the next level. All of these examples started with understanding the business, and then accelerated or pivoted after identifying the best route to growth. Innovation paired with execution is at the core of every evolving business.

BLUE OCEAN OFFERINGS

The book *Blue Ocean Strategies* by Chan Kim and Renee Mauborgne examines the strategic business models of companies that merge two standard offerings together to form something completely unique. By doing so, companies such as Cirque de Soleil, for example, avoid the competitive and bloody red waters and move into a wide-open "blue ocean" territory.

Consider the acquisition entrepreneur who acquired an art frame manufacturing company. After he made the purchase, with the initial goal of improving internal operations, he obverted his various customer markets and complementary purchases. He was able to identify an enormous opportunity to offer hospitals art consulting and design services, along with the custom framing manufacturing he already did. This expanded his current offering to fill an additional customer need, expanding the company into "blue ocean" territory.

UNDERSTANDING INNOVATION

Often, entrepreneurship is often associated with disrupting existing industries with innovation. In Clayton Christensen's book *The Innovator's Dilemma*, the Harvard professor beautifully illustrates the relationship between existing and disruptive technologies through mapping the quality level of the product over time. Mature markets often operate at a quality level above what is required by customers, eliminating quality issues between competitors, while emerging technologies are usually ignored by industry incumbents because the quality level is too low for offering to existing customers. As a result, it could actually have a negative impact on the reputation of the company.

Let's look at the digital camera in relation to Christensen's measurement tool. When it first came out, the quality of the pictures was low. They were grainy, and the industry giants, including Kodak, laughed in the face of the new technology. Then of course, with advances in technology, the digital camera moved in to eat Kodak's lunch and dominate the field, which is the trend in disruption.

Products creep into the market that don't necessarily serve the needs of the whole population, but eventually, they move in to replace the "sustainable" existing product. I love Christensen's graph because the inventory of businesses available for acquisition fall almost exclusively above the top line, which is where most entrepreneurs want to be.

"But don't we want to start the disruptive technology?" you ask. According to Jim Collins in *How the Mighty Fall*, incumbents have a higher likelihood of sustainability and domination within their industries than newcomers. The existing companies that can make the leap dominate the new entrants, even in the newly defined market.

An example of an acquisition entrepreneur capitalizing on growth through adopting disruptive technologies and offering them to current customers can be found in St. Louis. By acquiring three smaller companies in the IT services sector, one former classmate of mine ended up building one of the largest datacenters in the Midwest. The firms he bought weren't doing anything particularly remarkable, but they were filling a need and had paying customers. Eventually, they expanded by adding additional services to address existing customer needs. Along the way, he made the expensive and important decision to build massive server infrastructure, supporting the investment by offering cloud and colocation services to existing customers. Today, he operates datacenters in three major cities and supports some of the biggest brands in the country. All because he took an existing business and listened to the customers in order to develop an entirely new disruptive offering.

The Innovator's Dilemma is a great way to evaluate the disruptive offerings threatening an industry, but it's not always the path to the fast growth the infamous disruptive companies experience. There's a different tool box for that.

THE UNICORN TOOL BOX

Well then, what tools might we look to in order to create an innovative, fast-growing company? In *Exponential Organizations,* Salim Ismail says organizations that are growing exponentially (the unicorns) have adapted to the technologies that are growing exponentially. They don't allow the business to be a bottleneck for growth, and it's possible to go from startup to a Fortune 500 company faster than ever before.

Ismail and his team at Singularity University reverse engineered a menu of common denominators high-growth companies share. They have effectively created a blueprint for designing the organization of the future. Ismail outlines eleven elements that are optional for an "ExO,"[74] but the inclusion of only *some of them* is required for success. One of the components is leveraging existing assets, one of

---

74   *https://backchannel.com/here-are-the-secrets-of-unicorn-companies-c8951b99215b#.*
     jyrnxnp7m

the core principles of acquisition entrepreneurship.

Similarly, Robert Goldberg, managing partner of GTG Capital and former Zynga executive, helped the company close forty acquisitions over two and a half years. He drove Zynga's growth from thirty to 30,000 in that same timeframe—making it one of the fastest growing companies of all time. At his private equity firm, he utilizes the elements as observed by Ismail and implements them into small to mid-sized companies in an effort to realize a minimum of doubling the current growth rates. He acquires the companies fully only after he's able to see evidence of success in doubling growth the rate.

What Goldberg is doing is no secret: he's building tremendous value within organizations that already have revenue, infrastructure, and earnings. He is anchored in the philosophy of "keeping one foot in the new economy and one foot in the practical economy," thereby proving that disruption and exponential growth are not reserved exclusively for startups. Masterful acquisition entrepreneurs can experience explosive growth from small businesses in mature industries. Goldberg is living proof.

PRODUCT SUBSCRIPTIONS

Finally, John Warrilow, author of *Built to Sell* and *The Automatic Customer*, creates step-by-step instructions to create a product offering from a service, and a subscription model from a product offering. By executing this, companies can drive growth through unique positioning in the marketplace and increase company value exponentially by applying a subscription model.

The tools and frameworks in this chapter might be too much to consider. Or they might shed light on the single best opportunity the company has to create tremendous value. As the new CEO, the call is yours.

Once your vision and business plan are put together, it's time to acquire the company. The next chapter will walk you through the step-by-step process of buying an existing company and executing your dream of practicing entrepreneurship through acquisition.

PART 4

EXECUTION

"To hell with circumstances; I create opportunities."

—Bruce Lee

CHAPTER 10

MAKING AN OFFER

UNDERSTANDING THAT EACH ACQUISITION IS UNIQUE TO ITSELF, there are still events, tasks, and milestones to the process that are common among all transactions. This process begins with much of what we covered in the first parts of this book: commitment, preparation, and the search.

Since you have now identified an acquisition target that meets your target statement, it's time to make an initial offer. This comes in the form of a Letter of Intent to Purchase (LOI). This is the time when you make an offer, including the price, terms, and structure of the deal. Once agreed to, the LOI will provide the necessary understanding of the deal needed to move forward in the acquisition process.

PHASES OF ACQUISITION

Figure 10.1: The Acquisition Process

LETTER OF INTENT

An LOI can also be called a "term sheet" or "Memorandum of Understanding" (MOU). By any name, these documents are essentially the same thing: a non-binding agreement that outlines the price, structure, and terms of your offer.

The presentation of the LOI is typically the time when negotiations begin. The good news is that the Letter of Intent is a high-level document. Many of the details are put off until the construction of a Purchase Agreement later in the process. The benefit is it allows you to get on the same page as the seller and move forward with the process before getting hung up in the details.

There are seven main points common to an LOI. Often, the broker will even have a formatted LOI that you can use, but not always. Of course, we also have examples on *BuyThenBuild.com*. Here are the common points:

- The type of the purchase you propose (asset or stock sale)
- The purchase consideration, or how much you are offering to pay and when (i.e. the structure)
- A date of closing, typically six to eight weeks out
- Any contingencies you require
- Agreement to sign an Asset Purchase Agreement in the future, typically prior to closing and based on the terms outlined in the LOI
- An outline of an escrow deposit you will make if the LOI is accepted
- An outline of expenses each party will be responsible for in the process
- Confidentiality and exclusivity

That's it!

Because an LOI is a *non-binding agreement,* I want you to get comfortable with taking the step of making an offer. Too many potential buyers want to spend time doing more research and use it as an excuse to not move forward. It's certainly okay to request the information you need to make a decision about whether to make an offer, but the pre-LOI phase is not the time to do due diligence. Either you like the business enough to move forward, or you don't. Make a decision.

I'll borrow from David Sandler and say it's either a "real yes," a "real no," or "real next steps." While looking at a potential acquisition, I want you to always look back at the phases of acquisition outlined above and continually move forward—or walk away. Remember, at any point in the process before closing, you can decide the deal is not a fit for you. In the same regard, a seller might decide not to sell to you or sell at all. Keeping the deal moving forward is the way to ensure you will reach your goal.

The LOI only outlines the terms of the deal you will make in the future, it's okay to move forward with very limited legal counsel at this stage;[75] you're just putting terms down to see if you can reach an agreement. So be comfortable with this step—you're not buying the business yet. Often, many move forward with an LOI even without legal counsel. Again, it's non-binding, so buyers can put this together with the assistance of a broker or a boiler plate form from their lawyer. Just make sure you actually mean what you

---

75 I just made every lawyer in the world cringe. Do your homework, understand your legal responsibilities and risks at every stage, and decide for yourself how protected you want to be at every step. I am only sharing with you how I perceive and typically move forward at the LOI stage. In my opinion, this is not the time to run up legal fees; this is a largely non-binding document that is a written discussion between you and the seller.

propose and you are willing to move forward should it be accepted.

Good businesses sell quickly as well. Offering the seller an LOI for consideration is the best way to know if you will be the favored buyer or not. I have submitted plenty of LOIs that were rejected by the seller due to the seller taking more attractive offers. Moving quickly at the beginning communicates to the seller that you are a *real* buyer with intent to purchase and, if accepted, ensures that the deal will move forward and, if closed, that you are the buyer.

The other benefit of moving toward an LOI is that it forces you to think through the characteristics of the offer you'd like to make.

Although you have been looking at many companies up to this point, it is critical that you understand you should only have one Letter of Intent active at any given time. This is because the LOI is akin to a marriage engagement or an offer on a house—you are intending to move forward with this one major life decision: to buy this company. Once an LOI is accepted, you should stop shopping other opportunities and focus on getting the deal completed.

Let's address each of the LOI points outlined above one at a time.

ASSET VERSUS STOCK SALE

At the point of LOI, you'll want to indicate whether you are proposing an asset sale or a stock sale. An asset sale is simply that—you are a separate entity, acquiring the assets of the target company. A stock sale means you are buying the actual legal entity.

ASSET SALE

The vast majority of lower middle-market transactions are asset sales. This is good for the buyer because it is what you want. First, you aren't adopting any risk associated with historical behavior of the seller; instead, you will form a new legal entity and acquire the assets of the company in order to perform the operations. You'll assign a "doing business as" (DBA) status with your entity so that it is able to continue operating under the same brand as the company you are buying. This structure means you are not liable for anything that happened prior to the date of the acquisition. It's a fresh start for everyone involved.

Most importantly, you are not acquiring any of the liabilities the current business has in an asset sale. Any long-term debt on the balance sheet is assigned to the seller, as well as the cash. You'll be applying your own long-term liabilities to your new balance sheet (i.e. bank debt) and have the benefit of depreciating the assets you buy at a negotiated value. The exact value of these assets will be assigned later (usually by agreements driven between the professionals on both sides: the accountants and the lawyers), and you don't need to propose anything to do with this at the LOI stage.

STOCK SALE

Every once in a while, there is a need to execute a stock sale instead of an asset sale. This could be due to a specific, value-driving contract or license that the company has that isn't transferrable or is difficult or impossible to attain otherwise.

Note that stock sales greatly benefit the seller in terms of taxes saved as a result of the sale, so if an intermediary suggests a stock sale, it's fine as a suggestion. However, make absolutely sure that you agree. In the same regard, your offer may be able to be lowered because of the additional benefit to the seller's pocket.

If you need to execute a stock sale, it is absolutely critical that you get the best possible legal representation authoring the indemnification clauses. A stock sale can really take the "two people working toward a common goal" approach and move it to a "buyer's protection at any and all costs" position. I also recommend a hefty seller financial investment in the future of the company, either through significant financing or some major holdback granted to them at a later date. This will allow you as the buyer to have significant influence on the seller's actions in the event you do need it.

The bottom line is that this book takes the approach that you are an acquisition entrepreneur looking to buy a business in the lower middle market. Because of this, it should be assumed that you will be offering and closing on an asset sale, with few exceptions.

PURCHASE CONSIDERATION (OR, HOW MUCH TO OFFER)

A lot goes into your proposed purchase price: your own valuation from the exercise in Chapter 7, the asking price from the Offering Memorandum, what assets you include in the purchase, and the deal structure you're proposing.

As you consider making an offer, I want you to compare your estimated valuation to the asking price. I directed you earlier to ignore it. This was because it's impossible for you to determine your own valuation if you are considering the asking price as factual from the beginning.[76]

But here's where this becomes important. The asking price is the valuation the seller has gotten comfortable with. Likely, when they first explored selling, they learned that their original idea of what their company was worth was tremendously overvalued. From there, they worked with an advisor to understand the market, current day multiples for companies like theirs, and in the end agreed

---

76 In fact, many lower middle-market companies are brought to market without prices at all in order to focus specifically on what the value of the company is to the buyer.

to list the price with this valuation. So, mentally, this is what they are prepared to sell for.

Just like residential homes, the company might sell for below, at, or above the asking price. And just like residential homes, it might be really close or it might be a significant deviation one way or the other.

However, before deciding what you want to offer, there is another critical step you need to complete. You need to stress test your investment so you can get comfortable with the downside risk associated with your investment.

STRESS TEST

To stress test your model, simply consider the burden of the loan on discretionary earnings and then consider how much revenue would need to *decrease* in order for you to get into trouble. Let's walk through an example.

Say SDE is $400,000 annually and you're going to pay a 3.2 multiple on this amount, or a $1.2 million purchase price. You require another $100,000 for inventory and $100,000 in working capital, for a total $1.4 million at closing. You decide you're going to finance 90 percent of this acquisition, or $1.26 million at a 6 percent, ten-year loan.

This loan will cost approximately $168,000 annually, which leaves $232,000 in current SDE available.

You decide that even in the worst of times you need to either make $80,000 in annual salary or hire a manager at that amount to run the company. This means that the company can maintain the debt and labor at an SDE of no less than $248,000 ($168,000 in principal and interest payments plus $80,000 in management fees).

Since SDE is running about 15 percent at the company currently, its revenues are approaching $2.7 million. At a stressed SDE of $248,000, it's revenues would only be $1.7 million, representing a 37 percent decline in revenue.

Do you feel comfortable that you can continue to grow the company? Or that the company won't go below a 37 percent drop in revenue in a downturn? If that were to happen, what expenses could be cut?

Obviously, you are not buying a company because of the risk of a downturn, but it's critical to understand the calculated risk you are taking and think through the worst-case scenario. You'll be thinking through the best-case scenario when forecasting what you plan to do with the company, so this exercise goes both ways.

WHAT'S INCLUDED

Make sure you understand what the asking price includes. Anything with SDE under $2 million will likely be listed as an asset sale. As the buyer, you absolutely want this, except in rare circumstances. The reason is because when you buy assets, you are buying all of the infrastructure that generates the profitable revenue, without accepting the risk of anything they've done in the past. Further, you're not taking on any of the long-term debt associated with the prior ownership.

An asset sale typically does not include anything you may associate with working capital, such as cash, inventory, accounts receivable (AR), or accounts payable (AP). You'll want to look at these and have a firm understanding of what you are buying. You get very precise with these numbers as closing approaches, but my rules of thumb look like this:

Cash

Don't buy their cash. Why would you buy cash? It doesn't make sense. The seller will walk with all their cash and all their debt so that the balance sheet will be recreated as a new company under your ownership.

Inventory

Don't buy any outdated or unusable inventory. Personally, I don't acquire inventory in excess of what I'd expect to use in the first ninety days of ownership. In some cases I have paid for more, but this is when the owner doesn't want to remove it and they'll accept selling it for a fraction of what it's worth.

Accounts Receivable and Accounts Payable

After studying the AR and AP reports and talking to the seller, you'll get a sense of anything too old. I don't like buying any AR over sixty days, but if it looks like they will eventually pay, I'll accept the older AR with a contingency that the seller is on the hook for it if the customer doesn't pay.

I do accept the AP, because AR minus AP is the bulk of working capital in the business. The seller will be incentivized to get inventory to a manageable position and get AP to as close to zero as possible. They'll also prefer to turn any AR into cash, but only mildly because, at closing, good AR is the same as cash to them. As a buyer, you are okay with all of this because it lowers short-term debt and increases healthy, manageable working capital.

Key Assets

You are buying all assets of the company necessary to continue operations and the corresponding cash flow. This is precisely the infrastructure you are after. Ultimately, just make sure you're getting the assets you need to continue the operations of the business. If in doubt, include it. The details behind this section will really come into play during the purchase agreement. At the LOI stage, it's simply listed that you are buying all assets of the business in good, working condition.

Real Estate

I didn't mention this above because it's not a working capital component, but it does belong here as a consideration on your offer. Personally, my default setting is that, although I like real estate investments, I prefer to keep them separate from business investments. This is for two reasons. First, the drivers of a real estate investment are typically different from a business investment. Said another way, the characteristics of an attractive acquisition target have nothing at all to do with the real estate associated with it. There is no reason to acquire an asset that isn't directly related to the generation of profitable revenue. Further, since the business you are acquiring is the tenant of this property, it's an undiversified investment for you, tying the building directly to your business investment.

Second, if you are planning on growing or changing the business in any way to fit your vision, you may wish to leave the location for a more favorable location sometime down the line. You don't want to be making business decisions based on real estate investments.

If the owner owns the building and is offering it for sale, their biggest concern is that you will not want to use the real estate at all and will buy the business and move somewhere else, leaving them with an empty building. This costs them money instead of making them money. You likely don't want to do this either.

As a result, it's common to address it by agreeing to a three- to ten-year lease, with the option to purchase the building at the end of the term. This is ideal for you as the buyer because, after you run the business for three to five years, you will know whether the real estate makes for a good investment opportunity, depending on the tenant—you!

Taking what's included in the asking price into consideration, you can understand what your offer should likely include. An asset sale with X offer price, plus inventory, plus AR, minus AP. This is the most common approach.

DEAL STRUCTURE

Although there are seemingly unlimited ways to structure an acquisition based on the details of the variables involved, there are three primary approaches: all cash, earnout, and purchase with a seller note. Your LOI will outline your proposed deal structure.

There are three reasons why an all-cash offer[77] could come into play. The first is that you absolutely love the business, have absolute confidence in its ability to continue on a positive trajectory, and wish to offer an all-cash offer in order to reduce your purchase price. This will allow the seller to walk away at closing with 100 percent of the money from exiting the business.

The second is due to a very good business for sale that is anticipated to sell quickly. I've made all-cash offers to purchase companies that have been rejected because they received higher all-cash offers from known good buyers. This has happened to me more than once and has helped give me insight that the lower middle market is a seller's market. Moving quickly and offering fair offers can be absolutely essential if you see a business that meets your criteria. However, I want to caution against a "bidding war" with other

---

77 Note that an all-cash offer doesn't mean there is no financing involved. I always recommend that a contingency of the buyer should include the need to obtain financing. All-cash, in this instance, simply means that the seller walks away from closing with 100 percent of the purchase price and nothing material owed to them.

potential buyers—where you increase your offer and they increase theirs, driving the price up. Just remember, you haven't done due diligence yet. You have an idea of what the business is, but anything can happen in the due diligence phase.

Whenever I get in this situation, I simply stay in contact with the buyer during due diligence, just letting them know that I am interested should the deal fall apart in due diligence. If you miss out on an opportunity because of another buyer, just be patient. There are plenty of businesses out there and another one that fits your criteria will arise.

Having an all-cash offer puts buyers at a disadvantage since they accept all the risk from the seller on day one. There are many ways to finance an acquisition, and the SBA is just one of them. If you can obtain a commercial loan with a fixed rate and no personal guarantee, that is the ideal form of financing. It will also allow you more freedom in structuring your proposal.

Earnouts keep the risk of the company with the seller even though the buyer is taking over ownership. Most of the time, a seller will not be open to this, but there are a few instances where an earnout is the textbook solution to the deal structure. This is often when there is a material risk or real material reward in the near future. Note, if you are planning on using an SBA loan, they don't currently allow for a 100 percent earnout structure, so you'll need a different method of financing.

In other words, if the company is trending downward and it appears like it will continue, it is appropriate for the seller to accept an earnout based on future performance, since it looks like it will be worth less in the near future. The same is true for the opposite—if the company appears to have a solid growth opportunity around the corner, an earnout would allow for the owner to reap some of the benefits of their work. High customer concentration[78] or a large contract coming up for renewal are characteristics that add risk for the buyer and can be addressed with an earnout. Essentially, earnouts are a way to address potential and substantial changes to company performance in the near future. The better the performance of the business, the more likely an earnout is not an option for a buyer. However, this does not mean that good opportunities, or more importantly, the right opportunity for you won't include one. Undervalued companies that require your skillset as the driver for value increase are precisely where this could come into play, or with companies growing through acquisition.

Having the seller carry a note is the absolute best way to approach most acquisitions. The reason is because either the seller gets paid in full per your agreement, or more typically, gets the business *back* from you should you fail to pay. This means that they are taking on risk associated with you and your ability to perform in the business.

A typical structure is that the amount of the note, associated interest, and payment schedule are agreed to, then paid out by the company over, say, two to five years. A typical seller note would be 10 to 20 percent of the purchase price paid out at a lower interest rate over the following few years. As a result, the seller is actually helping you finance the purchase. Further, the bank might consider the seller note as equity, and not even require you to come up with any initial capital. If you want to buy a business with no money down, this is probably the most common strategy.

---

78 High customer concentration refers to a single or a few customers representing a significant portion of revenue.

CLOSING DATE

This is the date you are proposing to close. A fast close will be a favorable deal point to the seller. In the same regard, once the current owner decides to sell, I find I prefer to get in as soon as possible. There are three reasons for this:

First, time kills all deals, and if you can close quickly you increase the odds of closing.

Second, once the owner decides to sell and they have a signed LOI, they are no longer nearly as engaged with the business. Performance typically suffers.

Third, you already decided to purchase it, right? It's time to get through the rest of the process and get to work. If anything is off in due diligence, you'll be able to stop and reevaluate.

Set the closing date out far enough that you can secure financing and complete due diligence, plus about ten days. If there are delays, the buyer and seller can reevaluate along the way and decide whether to recommit to each other. This time period is typically thirty to ninety days out, depending on the size and complexity of the transaction.

CONTINGENCIES

You should include any contingencies you require in the LOI. Typically, this will include things like the buyer's ability to obtain financing, a satisfactory completion of due diligence, and when that period ends. Every situation is different, so predicting the unique contingencies in any situation can't be done here. Instead, let's review some of the more common contingencies:

BUYER'S ABILITY TO OBTAIN FINANCING

This contingency essentially says that if you, the buyer, are unable to obtain financing to purchase the business using the assets as collateral, then you are not required to buy said business. This point is critical for the buyer, but it is the first contingency sellers will want removed because it's the number one thing out of their control in the whole contract.

SATISFACTORY COMPLETION OF DUE DILIGENCE

This section explains that you'll be using outside professionals to assist in due diligence and that you'll need access to everything you can think of, from insurance policies and employee benefit programs to inventory and financial records. Other contingencies in the LOI will outline proactive requests for specific information, but this section is your approval for access to anything you may need.

Perhaps most important, you will indicate the end time of the due diligence period here. You have the right to due diligence, but the seller has a right to know, at the very least, a couple weeks before closing whether your due diligence period ended "satisfactorily." In other words, you are maintaining the right to change the terms of the deal based on your findings in the due diligence period.

ACCESS TO CONTRACTS

You are proactively asking the seller for any and all contracts so you are able to review them. You will also require the seller to take any action necessary to obtain successful assignment of these contracts to your entity prior to (or at the time of) closing.

TAX RETURNS

You may have requested tax returns prior to this stage, but odds are you were able to make a decision to offer an LOI based on what was supplied. This section specifically breaks out the fact that you need tax returns from the prior three to five years, plus all W-2s, 1099s, and payroll records for the most recent year.

NON-COMPETE

Of course, you will absolutely require the seller sign a non-compete so that they don't open a competing company and approach your newly acquired customers. A reasonable non-compete would ask for three to five years in the same industry in a specific geographic region or sector.

SELLER TRAINING

I always ask for ninety days on site. In practice, it will typically last one to four weeks part time. Still, having the ability to have committed cooperation beyond a thirty-day period should be a requirement. Getting the seller to commit to ninety days is more insurance than anything else. I am also of the mind that this is not a difficult ask for the seller to agree to. I always require an additional six months available by phone. This firmly sets my expectations and doesn't leave any loose ends.

INTERVIEWS WITH KEY EMPLOYEES, SUPPLIERS, OR CUSTOMERS

In certain situations, you will absolutely want to have open conversations with key personnel or management to ascertain their interest in staying on. This is also true of key suppliers and key customers. The latter is the most difficult from the seller's perspective. Open discussions with customers or clients before closing is the maximum amount of risk a seller could take. Still, certain situations absolutely require this from the seller's side. You'll need to work out an appropriate solution that you are comfortable with.

The time the seller will agree to these types of meetings will be at the very end of the process, just prior to closing, and only after all financing has been committed and due diligence has been completed satisfactorily. If not, typically an earnout or holdback should be enough to compensate for the risk you are taking.

APPRAISAL OF COMPANY

The bank will require an appraisal of the company in order to supply financing, so the seller's cooperation is required.

REAL ESTATE CONSIDERATIONS

If there is real estate involved in the transaction, there will need to be an appraisal done as well as any other required due diligence, such as an environmental report, for example. If the asset is not being purchased, the closing must be contingent upon a lease agreed to and signed at closing.

DISCLOSURES INCLUDING ANY KNOWN LITIGATION

Imagine the seller is aware they are being sued and they don't tell you. Or a big customer is leaving, and they fail to mention it. Yep, you need to know this stuff. Closing is contingent on full disclosure.

EQUIPMENT WILL BE IN GOOD WORKING ORDER

Remember, you're buying earnings that are provided by the infrastructure of the company. You need to know the exact state of all that infrastructure, but the minimum viable requirement of this is knowing that the equipment will work on day one.

ASSET PURCHASE AGREEMENT

Closing will be contingent on the buyer and seller being able to work out and agree to a finalized and binding purchase agreement. This is typically needed before closing for financing purposes more than anything else. It also helps minimize last-minute surprises or changes. Setting expectations and meeting expectations will be critical through the entire process.

AGREEMENT TO AN AGREEMENT, ESCROW, AND EXPENSES

These sections simply outline some of the typical legal agreement details.

There will be a binding purchase agreement that is based on the terms outlined in the LOI prior to closing. You are effectively agreeing that you intend to move forward with signing when the time comes and based on mutual agreement of the terms.

You will make an escrow deposit with the broker in a specific amount if the LOI is accepted. This is commonplace and holds your feet to the fire only later in the game. If something goes south prior to the end of the due diligence phase, you will get this money back. I recommend you discuss this with the broker to get a feel for what is appropriate.

The expenses section more or less outlines that each of you will have a lawyer and that each party is responsible for paying their legal representation.

CONFIDENTIALITY, EXCLUSIVITY, AND NON-BINDING STATEMENTS

As we've pointed out repeatedly, the LOI is a non-binding document. Except for one part. Once agreed to, the seller has signed on with you for an exclusive period, meaning they can't market the company to other potential buyers. By signing an LOI, they effectively take the business off the market and they are now committed to you as the buyer for a defined period (maybe sixty days). This is a critical observation because the seller is investing in you as a buyer. I like to respect this decision on their part, understanding that the next sixty days or so are a critical time for all parties, and it's time to get going on constructing the purchase agreement and due diligence. The confidentiality agreement is also fully enforced on both sides (or, if not mutually agreed upon, you'll see larger buyouts announced in the trades after an LOI occurs), and it will include a statement making clear that it is, in fact, a non-binding agreement. At times the first document will be submitted as a legally binding document, so make sure the language fits what you are trying to accomplish.

When you've successfully put your LOI together, submit it to the intermediary, never to the seller. It is a requirement that the intermediary present all offers to the seller. When the time comes to present the LOI to the intermediary, you have likely had a minimum of a few conversations with them and they know what to expect.

The email in which you send the LOI, or perhaps the LOI itself, will also contain a deadline. After you submit your LOI, it's time to wait. Do nothing until the deadline has been hit. Do not contact the broker; do not contact the seller. Simply remove yourself from the equation and let them work through it, lest you open yourself up to piecemeal negotiations.

PRE-NEGOTIATION APPROACH

When making an offer via LOI, you need to consider your negotiation strategy. In general, there are two approaches. You can either offer a price based on your own valuation of the company with the intent of sticking close to it; or, you can offer a price substantially below the asking price and play "hardball" to get the lowest price possible.

This will be mostly up to your style, but I prefer, and recommend, the former. This goes back to a fundamental belief that the
buyer and the seller are two people moving toward a common goal.
Remember, you don't have to buy anything. In the same regard, the
seller can decide they don't want to sell. Maintaining the partnership toward a common goal means not being overly-aggressive,
combative, or unreasonable during negotiations.

There are a lot of benefits to coming in with a real offer from
the beginning. First, the seller will acknowledge you are a real buyer.
Often, a fair offer paired with the decision to make one quickly
will be the "bird in hand" on a new, good listing. Good listings sell
quickly, and if you're wanting to spend a bunch of time positioning
and making perceived low-ball offers, the seller can move on to
another fair offer, knowing it's not going to be a battle all the way
through the process. Establishing yourself as someone they want
to work with is extremely beneficial.

Second, assuming the price you will pay is in the proper valuation range, the burden you pay will be based more on the structure
of the deal you propose than the amount. Are you addressing what's
important to them? How much cash is up front? Is there a seller
note or an earnout? Is it all cash? Wiggling the deal structure wig-
gles the price you pay.

Also, it's possible the asking price of the business is legitimately overpriced. This doesn't mean that the price doesn't pass
a stress test, that's a separate data point. However, sometimes a
seller will compare multiple brokers before listing. Sometimes, the
broker with the highest listing price (not the most realistic asking
price) will get the listing. If the asking price is too far off, you can
either walk away, or if you have a lot of time invested, you may
choose to have a conversation with the broker along the lines of

if-I-were-to-make-an-offer-it-would-look-like-this type of conversation. If the broker encourages you to make the offer, you can, but don't be too invested in the result.

SELLER RESPONSE TO THE LOI

The odds of the seller agreeing to the initial LOI depends on how close your offer is to their expectations (i.e. the asking price, assuming there is one). It's not the norm for an LOI to be accepted on a first round unless you offered the asking price at minimum, or perhaps have no need for a financing contingency and can close quickly. The one time I bought a company based on an accepted first offer was because a key person was leaving and the seller wanted out in the next forty-five days. The driver for his exit was speed, not price.

Typically, however, there will be some back and forth to reach an agreement. But know that once an LOI is submitted to the seller, the odds that you will continue to move forward is significantly improved over previous stages of the acquisition process.

The broker will reach out to you with the seller's response. It will either be an acceptance, a rejection, or a counteroffer. The counteroffer being the most common response. Let's review each one.

ACCEPTANCE

Usually, if the seller accepts the initial offer, the first thing that a buyer thinks is that their offer was too high. Don't concern yourself with these counterproductive thoughts. Instead, understand that you are an extremely prepared buyer, you know what you're looking for, you've done your valuation, and you've made an offer likely very close to that. The seller is probably thinking the broker listed it too low.

REJECTION

Typically, this happens either because your offer was too low in the seller's eyes, or they received multiple offers and accepted a different one. Assuming the former, total rejection with no counteroffer usually comes with a statement along the lines of "the seller was insulted by your offer," or something similar. Well, your offer is based off data, market conditions, and calculating a price that the company can afford. Often, either the seller has unrealistic expectations or the broker's asking price is too high. Sometimes the seller just decides they no longer want to sell at that price. More likely, the seller just requires more to feel like they are exiting at a fair deal for them. If it's total rejection without a counteroffer, it's because you're too far apart.

All is not lost, but the play here is to call the advisor and understand why. The advisor will want to help you. I like to listen for the drivers of the seller's decision and see if I can get creative around the solution. Ongoing income can result from seller financing, upside can result from an earnout, maybe they want to retain a portion of the business, or maybe they need to unload the real estate. Or, maybe you're just too far apart, and that's fine.

Following rejection, I'm typically open to making one more final offer, but understand that it's unlikely they'll accept. Either that or they are bringing a win-lose approach to the deal and it will be very difficult to work with them through the balance of the process, which is not at all worth it. You should consider the seller's needs, but above all only make offers that are right for you.

Rejection can also come quickly if you are working with companies that are not actively listed for sale. With the first few companies I attempted to buy, the owner simply had unrealistic expectations. A broker had not worked with them to coach them through the initial stages of the market for their size of a company. Since many owners believe their business is worth way more than it is, I quickly encountered a series of owners who wanted twenty-times EBITDA for companies all under $5 million in revenue. This is obviously not worth a counteroffer or even attempting to educate the seller. Targeting companies that are actively listed for sale can save you years.

COUNTEROFFER

A counteroffer is going to have edits to either the purchase price, the date of closing, the contingencies, or all three. Examine each point and look for where you have agreed. Hey, those are wins. Then try to understand the psychology of the seller. Are they wanting more cash at closing, a higher price, a faster closing? Typically, I take the approach that the more money they want, that's fine, as long as I have forever to pay it to them. I'm exaggerating to make the point that an increase in purchase price is likely possible, since payment terms can also be addressed, and seller notes can come into play.

Talk with the advisor and understand the seller's positioning. Once you've decided your counter, call the advisor and walk them through what to expect and what your reasoning is on each counter point. You want to give them the tools to coach the seller. You could try yourself, but at this stage, the seller will trust the advisor more since you have everything to gain.

A little back and forth is normal. Make sure that at each round of negotiation you are over communicating with the advisor and getting something in return every time you give. The art of negotiation is in identifying the things that are not critical to you but are critical to the other party, and vice versa. Just remember, your goal here is to get a fair deal; as long as it's in the realm of fair, you can't make a bad agreement. In the same regard, if there is anything wrong with the business, you'll find it in the next phase and can always renegotiate accordingly.

MOVING FORWARD

Once both parties agree and sign a Letter of Intent, it's time to really dig in. The next chapter will outline the next steps in acquiring your business.

CHAPTER 11

THE ACQUISITION PHASE

ONCE A LETTER OF INTENT TO PURCHASE IS AGREED UPON, THE deal will move into the *acquisition phase*. This a time when multiple tasks are being performed simultaneously. During this phase, negotiations are ongoing, and as we explained in Chapter 8, emotions can run high—especially for the seller. If navigated successfully, you will reach the closing and begin your role as CEO of your new, established company.

During the acquisition phase, a lot of things have to happen at once. There are no one-after-the-other steps where we can outline "do this then that." Specific to the size of the deal, your requirements and how the pieces come together will dictate the flow. It's also the phase where the stakes are the highest from the perspective of "the deal," and typically where things go sideways—at least once. As long as you go into this phase with knowledge of what to expect, you can navigate it successfully.

During the acquisition phase, a number of things need to happen:

The Purchase Agreement needs to be constructed, negotiated, and agreed upon.

1. The buyer needs to form a legal entity.

2. The buyer needs to get committed financing in place.

3. The seller will remove any and all contingencies in the agreement.

4. The purchase price needs to be allocated.

5. Due diligence needs to be executed to a satisfactory level.

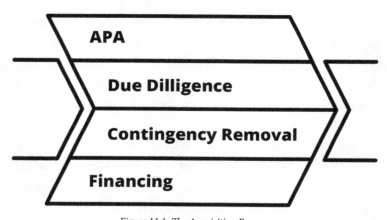

Figure 11.1: The Acquisition Process

We will review all of these, but first, let's understand the landscape of the acquisition phase.

COMMUNICATION CHANNELS

Part of what makes the acquisition phase challenging is the number of communication channels. You are talking with the broker and the seller. Sometimes on a conference call, and often one to one. You're talking with your accountant and your lawyer and potentially an investor. The seller has her lawyer and accountant, and so on. Perhaps the lawyers are in communication with each other or the accountants. Is the lender talking with the advisor? All in all, there will be a minimum of eight people involved, which equates to twenty-eight individual communication channels, which introduces exponential complexity to the equation.

First ask yourself, *What is the financial incentive of each person?*

The buyer: To buy a company. Probably the one they have under LOI, but maybe not.

The seller: To sell their specific company under certain conditions.

The broker: To do right by the seller and close a transaction.

The banker: To make a good loan. One that will get paid off in full and with interest.

Your accountant: To help you in the due diligence process and wave big red flags if they see things that are "off."

The lawyers: To protect their client at all costs, including not closing a deal for unreasonable conditions. The introduction of lawyers will, in my opinion, complicate agreements beyond what is necessary. This is because their job is to protect their client at all costs, no matter what happens, and will kill the deal if that's what needs to happen. This does not mean all lawyers will do this or that they are evil by nature; rather, it's critical you understand their incentive, because managing your legal counsel will be part of your tasks at this stage.

At the same time, it's often the representations and warranties—the exact binding clauses that protect a buyer—that overcomplicate the legal documents. Managing the right mix of protection versus getting the deal done should be up to you.

Adding these individual incentives on top of the twenty-eight communication channels, the emotional negotiation that will occur in this phase, and the probing due diligence process creates a complex and sensitive period. In speaking with advisors, they share that the closings that make them the most nervous are the ones that haven't fallen apart yet, because they all do at some point.

Just keep the goal in mind, stay true and firm to your point of view, be sensitive to the goals of all involved, and be reasonable. Getting ongoing progress with fair terms is your goal. The advisor should keep everything moving along because they know better than you that *time kills all deals*. Overcommunicate every step of the way.

IMMEDIATE ACTIONS

Immediately after getting a signed LOI, you need to take action on three fronts:

1. Begin paperwork with the bank to get the loan underwriting process underway. This has the biggest risk of being the bottleneck of the process, and you need to push for completion.

2. Communicate with your accountant and get a firm outline of everything they will need to assist you in due diligence so you can request it from the seller.

3. Call your lawyer and begin constructing a purchase agreement based on the agreed to LOI.

Do these things immediately, because they will take the longest to finalize of the deliverables. If you begin due diligence and find an issue, you'd rather find it with time to spare than down to the wire with no time to think.

CREATING YOUR BUSINESS ENTITY

Assuming your executing an asset purchase, you'll need to form a legal entity. This is fairly simple online, but you can recruit your lawyer should you choose to do so. You'll file with the state, submit a DBA request with the name of the business, open a bank account, and sign an operating agreement.[79] Check with your accountant regarding what type of entity is best for you.[80]

PURCHASE AGREEMENT

As we mentioned above, the complexities of an Asset Purchase Agreement (APA) are mostly due to the clauses that protect the buyer. These are the representations and warranties affiliated with what you're being told. You are relying on the seller to provide a true account of all information, supporting documents, financial information, and customer lists. It also forces disclosure of any potential issues. A valued customer potentially leaving, for example.

Whenever you begin a legal process between two parties, there is the decision of whether you want to pay the lawyer to draft the first proposed agreement or have the other party accept that expense and you deal with your attorney redlining the whole thing.

---

79 Either your lawyer can help with this or, for those DIYers out there, generic and executable operating agreements can be found online. If you are the sole owner, you may be able to get away with this. If you have partners, make sure the operating agreement is agreed to before you acquire a company.

80 Odds are it will be an LLC filing as an S-Corp.

Because the majority of complexity in an APA rests in protecting the buyer, I prefer to have my attorney draft the first iteration. This makes it so that every version going forward is impacting changes to the best possible version for myself as the buyer.

I coach the lawyer by explaining that the agreement is intended for two people to reach a common goal, not to protect me at all costs—something that could result in a one-sided document that can kill the deal. They always roll their eyes. Rightfully so. Their job is to protect me at all costs. However, from experience, I know that whatever my attorney produces will be returned from the seller's attorney covered in a bloodbath of red ink. In other words, it will be rewritten in the seller's favor. Just work through this step by step with the broker and the seller. Don't get overwhelmed with the lawyers making unrealistic demands. This is the root of the emotional reactions that occur in the acquisition phase. I encourage you to keep your cool and keep the end goal in mind.

The final APA will look a lot like the LOI, but instead of being a short, easy, one- to two-page document with a high-level understanding of payment, terms, and structure, it can be two dozen pages of details, complete with an abundance of appendices.[81] Multiple ongoing negotiations will occur as you move through resolutions of the details constructing the final APA.

Your legal counsel is a significantly better resource than this book to work with you on your purchase agreement. This is partially because they are your legal counsel, but also because efforts to standardize these types of documents have routinely failed, simply because of state-to-state variance in validity. An APA will include

---

81   In more Main Street type transactions, this document can be significantly simpler. Brokers typically have access to a blanket binding agreement that might be three to four pages plus appendices.

contents such as escrow arrangements, non-compete agreements, covenants, warranties, indemnifications, promissory notes, contingencies, a training period, and all other terms of the deal. There will also be schedules and exhibits outlining leases, contracts, supplier agreements, the closing balance of AR and AP, inventory records, customer lists, price sheets, hard asset and intangible asset lists, and anything else that is agreed to.

This document is binding, and it is here to protect you and the seller. Make sure every consideration is given regarding what you need to be true in order to buy the business. Unfortunately for the buyer, the APA is typically required in order to get bank financing, so you will be required to commit and sign it before closing, should you be using a method of financing such as the Small Business Administration.

ALLOCATION OF PURCHASE PRICE

Each dollar of the purchase price needs to be allocated to an asset that is being bought in the business for tax reasons. Both the buyer and the seller will report this to the IRS and what the money bought has different tax implications for each party. A new $25,000 ERP system that was fully depreciated via section 179 will want to be purchased at its full value by the buyer so they can depreciate it. The seller will have to pay income tax on that amount, since they already took the tax benefit of depreciating it.

It's relatively easy for the accountants to agree on the allocation of assets, but you will likely be negotiating portions of this as they come up. Make sure you discuss with your accountant how the allocation of purchase price impacts you so that you know the difference between where you want the allocation and where the seller will want the allocation. Common examples of allocation are:

- Inventory
- Furniture, Fixtures, and Equipment (FF&E)
- Non-Compete
- Office Supplies
- IP
- Goodwill

DUE DILIGENCE

Up until now, I've asked you to take a "trust but verify" approach to the evaluation and analysis of the acquisition target. Due diligence is permission to enter the verify portion. This is where all the assumptions, as well as everything you've been told by the seller and broker, come under investigation. You require validation that everything you've received is correct. If the advisor is a good one, the materials will have been very well put together and reviewed before they got to you. This does not mean that they don't need to be verified, it just means that things are clean, in order, and prepared. This will make the entire process easier.

Entire books have been written about due diligence, and you can often find extensive lists showing everything that a buyer will want to see. The lists can be quite lengthy and deliberately intimidating. I want to cover the broad strokes of the due diligence period in under 700 words so that you have plenty to get you started, and from which the momentum could be enough to carry you through the entire process.

Due diligence typically falls in three categories: legal, financial, and operational. In a small, easily verifiable business, due diligence can be completed over the course of a couple of hardworking weeks. Larger companies may require a full four-plus weeks. Either way, it's time to get under the hood and truly understand the business.

As we've discussed, acquisition entrepreneurship lies at the intersection of entrepreneurship and investing. Due diligence is the tool provided for you to evaluate the company as a potential investment. It's critical to get organized during this period because everything you review will result in more questions. Keep a to-do list or a project plan and make sure all your concerns can be addressed.

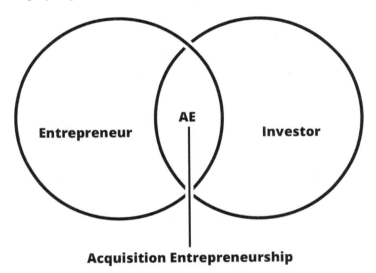

Acquisition Entrepreneurship

Figure 10.3: Acquisition Entrepreneurship is the intersection
of entrepreneurship and investing.

Begin with getting the legal and financial diligence underway. This is partially because you can outsource the majority of it, or at least get very specific guidance from your accountant and lawyer. The other reason is you can perform much of it before any technical due diligence period begins, which maximizes your time for review.

LEGAL DUE DILIGENCE

The legal aspects start at the beginning, making sure the entity is legal and the seller has the right to sell it to you. Certificates of incorporation, company operating agreements, by-laws, any and all agreements between partners, and proper licensing and permits with specific counties or states. From there it might move to supplier contracts, customer contracts, intellectual property rights, insurance contracts, and so on. Ultimately, you're validating the legitimacy of the business to do business, as well as any and all consequences resulting during the transition to you. Are there any current or pending legal issues?

FINANCIAL DUE DILIGENCE

Financial due diligence begins with validation that everything you've received is correct and ends with a deep understanding of the working capital of the business. You'll ask for internal statements, tax returns, monthly bank statements for the last three years, general ledgers, depreciation schedules, payroll records, updated statements from all major suppliers, owner's W-2s, and detailed lists of all equipment, inventory, and office supplies.

You'll need to assess any equipment, buildings, or other hard assets associated with the company. Ask yourself whether you require all of it. Get it assessed. Understand what equipment could break down and what the owner has done in the past if this occurs. Do they have proper maintenance records? Maintenance contracts? Who are the suppliers and what is the replacement cost?

The working capital required can be calculated by taking the current assets and subtracting the current liabilities from the balance sheet. Others prefer to have three months of operating expenses on hand, while some look at the Accounts Receivable

Aging report[82] and calculate how quickly inventory turns. None of these are wrong, but you should calculate all three and determine how long cash is typically tied up in the organization.

The goal of financial due diligence is to determine whether the numbers you find match what was presented to you. If so, great, you already have an agreement in place. If not, what has changed, how did it happen, and are you getting satisfactory information to identify what's wrong? Walking away or renegotiating the agreement is not off the table at any time before closing.

OPERATIONAL DUE DILIGENCE

Operational due diligence reviews how the entire operation of the business flows and works. Excellent brokers have advised me in the past that the best way to start is by following an order through the building. When a new order comes in, where does it start and how does it move its way through? It's proven an excellent exercise in getting the lay of the land quickly. You'll understand their internal systems, who's trained, who's key, and frankly, who's obsolete. You'll know where all the files are and can perform random checks on customer orders, accounts, and costs.

Operational due diligence also takes into consideration sales and marketing. What is the sales process? What do the sales people do? What marketing efforts are occurring? What's working and what's not? Did the owner cut back on marketing in order to increase SDE?

RABBIT HOLES

One of my business partners continually refers to due diligence as "running down the rabbit holes." It seems every question you

---

82 A report showing outstanding customer receivables and how long they have been past due.

ask will result in more questions rather than answers. Take time to get organized and thoroughly research everything that becomes a concern or is unclear to you. If you do this satisfactorily, it's possible you'll end with a better understanding of the business than the current owner, giving you confidence to effectively manage the business and move forward in the acquisition process quickly.

EXPLOITING OPPORTUNITIES

Some potential buyers get into the due diligence period and are simply looking for a reason not to do the deal. I suspect these are conservative investors who don't want to work that hard and, frankly, have not had the opportunity to do the prep work you have done. They've gotten this far and have started to experience buyer's remorse before they've even bought the company. I can't blame them. Due diligence is the time when you let your mind get negative, decide where the "snakes are hiding," and do your best to determine where you'll get screwed.

This is a good state of mind for this period, but recall that you are not only looking for holes in the story, but also validation of what you are buying. You need to learn the business, and this is the single best opportunity for you to learn the entire business with no risk other than your escrow deposit and professional fees. Use this time to examine and determine what the actual business drivers are, to determine whether this is a good business that you can make great with your skillset and effort. Keep in mind the words of Peter Drucker, who claimed, "Results are gained by exploiting opportunities, not by solving problems."

What's your greatest opportunity and what needs to be true in order for you to seize it?

REMOVING CONTINGENCIES

The contingencies outlined in the LOI will begin to be removed as fast as possible by the seller. The intermediary will be sure to move them forward on these tasks. These areas will include things like the lease, appraisals, approvals, permits and licenses, compliance, inventory, and AR and AP management and confirmation. It's critical that you do not close if the contingencies have not all been met.

In the same regard, the intermediary will want to remove your financing contingency as fast as possible and will be following up repeatedly with you to push that forward. The broker is doing exactly the right thing here because, as a representative of the seller, they know that the contingencies outside their control are the due diligence results and seller financing. Getting to a close means removal of those items, and the longer they are outstanding, the greater the risk the deal has of not closing.

THE NON-OWNER ADVANTAGE

After an LOI is agreed upon, most buyers turn heads-down into the financial and legal components of the business and the deal at hand. This is for very obvious and good reasons. However, I want to share that the time right in between a signed LOI and before due diligence truly gets under way is potentially the absolute best time to reach out to people in your network that might be potential customers.

This is because you don't own the business yet, so you can test the waters with zero risk. In other words, most people think sales people are trying to sell them something they don't need. Instead of erring on the side of caution, they'll be willing to help you with open arms. As a result, talking openly about what would need to be true for them to be future customers might result in them becoming future customers. If not, you'll get the advantage of great insights.

Once you own the business, you will have every incentive to sell them something, and they will know it. However, visiting with these people now, you don't have that risk. You're simply someone wanting to learn about the industry, the value that these types of companies provide, what the buyers look for, who the players in the industry are, even who the local individuals are who are influential in this space. It's a great opportunity to truly interview buyers and understand both the layout of the industry and the level of pain that the product or service relieves. I like to do a soft close at the end of these meetings. Say something like, "So, you said the value you get from these types of suppliers is X. If X were true at my company, would you consider switching?" This will tell you a lot about how commoditized the industry is and what the value drivers are.

You can use your sharpened networking skills from the search phase and reach out to people who own similar companies in different geographic areas as well.

Above all, however, respect the confidentiality agreement. The deal is not done until it's done, and the level of costly damage you could do to a seller is significant if things go a different direction. Leave your ego behind, be vague, and don't answer direct questions. You can communicate exactly what type of business it is and what service it provides without sharing the company or owner's name or where it is.

I consider this activity to be a third dimension of due diligence. It goes outside the normal structure and starts the foundation for success before the start gun fires. It can deepen your understanding of and insight into the industry even more than doing it immediately after the closing, which you will do as well.

PROGRESS

The acquisition phase is an exciting time and typically a bit of a roller coaster for all involved. Navigating these waters can be tricky and emotional at times, especially with all the people and incentives involved. But keep in mind the words of psychologist Timothy Pychyl: "We experience the strongest positive emotional response when we make progress on our most difficult goals." With every step you are getting closer to your goal of being a successful acquisition entrepreneur and the CEO of your own top-performing company.

By the time you are done with the acquisition phase and move into closing, you will be more comfortable with the business than you ever thought possible before starting down the acquisition entrepreneur road. Given how you've had a dedicated period to drill down everywhere you need to in order to satisfy every question or potential concern, you'll have insights into the company you couldn't have predicted, and as long as you've moved through the acquisition phase to your own satisfaction, you'll be feeling ready. More than that, you'll be excited and impatient to really get going at your new company.

It's time to close the deal.

CHAPTER 12

TRANSITION

CLOSING ON AN ACQUISITION IS NOT THE END OF THE BUYING process as much as it's the launch of your new entrepreneurial career. It's a nervous and exciting time.

If you are reading this chapter before going through the entire process in real life, then it may be hard to understand how well you'll know your new business at this point. If you took the due diligence process seriously and brought your hustle, you will have such an intimate understanding of the business that your clarity will give you a level of comfort with closing on it. You'll know the industry, competition, product, and have insight on the people inside the company. You're ready.

The reasons a buyer might not close should really only be two-fold. First, there was a material adverse change (MAC) in business performance during the acquisition phase; or second, you didn't complete your due diligence in the allotted time, so you felt uncertain.

MATERIAL ADVERSE CHANGE

Starting before the listing of the business went live, the seller likely went through a transition. They stopped running the company with full focus and started the exit process. Between that day and today, the business has changed. This is inevitable because businesses intrinsically have volatility. If the performance has slipped, this is to be expected. They've taken their eyes off the ball. If the performance difference is not "material," this is not the time to start renegotiating over a 5 percent drop. In the same regard, if there is a 5 percent increase, this is not the time for the seller to renegotiate with you. If the difference is significant enough, you should give consideration to changing the terms of the deal as early as possible, and well before the closing table.

DUE DILIGENCE

As we discussed, due diligence is the number-one best tool for buyers to learn the business. It's a defined period where buyers have free reign over any and all information. If you looked under every rock and ran down every rabbit hole, you're likely overprepared. There is no excuse to not complete due diligence effectively, so if you feel uncertain, this is likely your own fault. If, on the other hand, you feel uncertain because you don't trust the seller, you never should have gotten this far in the first place.

The night before, you'll be running through everything in your head. Wondering what you missed or how you might get the short end of the stick. This is normal. It's encouraged because there are bad situations out there. At the end of the day, you simply need to have enough information to know whether this is a sound business to buy. If so, you will be the CEO in a couple days' time and you will be able to manage business challenges as they come.

Buyers who fall out of the acquisition entrepreneur game fall out well before closing. They don't do the level of preparation you've done, they don't know what they're looking for in the first place, and they get overwhelmed or look for reasons not to take on any risk at all.

THE ELEVENTH HOUR FREAKOUT

Jason Yelowitz at Quiet Light Brokerage uses the term the *Eleventh Hour Freakout* to describe the common occurrence of buyers calling the broker as closing approaches with a new, heightened level of concern. As you, the buyer, move through understanding the business with new intimacy, you'll inevitably begin to see "how the sausage is made," and the allure that first attracted you may begin to wear off.

There might be a new discovery that pushes an existing concern to a new level. Or perhaps the persistent communication with the skeptics on your team, such as lawyers, accountants, and even your spouse, could put unnecessary weight on the risk you are about to take on.

Whatever the cause, know that this is common. Call the broker and work through your concerns. They are likely very manageable and nothing that can't be worked through. Or, perhaps they really are as serious as you think and you need to stop the deal from going through.

In that regard, this book gives you the framework that I have used to personally acquire over half a dozen companies over the last decade. Doing the appropriate prep work, including aligning the Three As and defining your target statement early on, are enough to carry you all the way through the process with confidence. The odds that your concerns need to shut down the entire process should be minimal, and only due to material adverse change.

You will still be nervous because you don't know what you don't know. That's true. Keep in mind that this is also true of every entrepreneur; and despite the unknown, we continue to take calculated risks, get after the goal, and create the future we wish to see.

This is your time.

CLOSING

Closing should start with all the closing documents being completed a few days prior to the closing date. Make sure you (or at least your attorney and the seller's attorney) have had an opportunity to review and approve them. This will reduce any surprises on closing day.

The day before closing is determining final inventory counts, along with the accounts receivable and accounts payable amounts. This is because not only do you need to know them, but they impact the total transaction price since they are typically in addition to the purchase price of the business itself. The inventory must be counted and priced. If the inventory is significant, you'll want to tackle this well in advance to the day before, or hire an inventory service to complete the count (and you then perform spot checks). My take on inventory is fairly straightforward. I buy anything that will be used in the first ninety days after closing, and I don't buy incomplete product.

What you want as a buyer is the inventory to match what you expected it to be. This is because if it is too high, you might not have secured enough financing to acquire it. On the other hand, if it's too low, you won't have enough inventory and you'll need to buy some quickly. This is the reason inventory is typically added as a separate line item at closing. If it were included, every seller would run inventory down as low as they could get it, which would put the business in a bad situation, risking the ability to fulfill orders. Throughout the process, keep advising the seller to run the business as if they weren't going to sell it. This will be the best way to assure everything is properly in place on day one.

Closing can be led by a neutral attorney, communication between your attorney and the seller's attorney, or the intermediary.

It can take place at the broker's office, your attorney's office, an accountant's office, the bank, or today, from the comfort of your own home (with a trip out to your bank to secure the loan).

The amount of paperwork is insurmountable. If you are using an SBA loan, be prepared for a twelve-inch stack of papers, including a personal guarantee, along with:

- Lease Agreement
- Agreement to Cooperate
- Lien filings
- Promissory notes
- Non-Compete Agreement
- Final inventory
- Final AR and AP

The lawyers will have prepared everything you could imagine. Make sure you get proper access to any IP, code, or virtual storage. The closing all ends with you accepting a Bill of Sale.

You may plan to be at the business by the end of the day to be introduced to the employees. In my experience, closing can take all day, and often it's the day after closing when you get to walk in as the new CEO.

HOW TO ESTABLISH YOURSELF AS THE NEW CEO

The first ninety days are a critical time to establish yourself with the employees, customers, and suppliers, get to know the internal systems and process, get a handle on cash flow, and begin to implement change.

Great integration starts in the planning phase before you close on the business. You've got a strategic plan and an idea where you want to take the company. These will serve as the north star, guiding your actions. But the first ninety days are truly spent in the weeds—the details of how the company functions.

It's important to set a goal or list objectives that are specific and achievable. This will focus your ability to prioritize. Keep in mind, the first couple of months will be spent mostly in a time of assessment, so your goals might be more qualitative at first. Confirm the company's strengths and weaknesses and the most critical people in the organization, and identify three ways to make internal systems more efficient, for example. This will start with the people and processes involved.

The seller will remain a part of the story for the first month. This will typically be transition oriented and involve training exercises. Once the sale is complete, a significant shift takes place in the relationship between the seller and the company. Even when there are financial incentives in place after the sale, most often, the seller's role within the organization has been replaced by you, which leads to the seller experiencing a lack of engagement with the business. For this reason, it's within everyone's best interests to have the seller leave within a brief, fixed amount of time. Do everything to ascertain their departure before the end of the first month. The sooner you keep them from coming to work, the better it will be for you.

Initiate an overall clean-up of the facility. Most small companies that have been owned by the same person or people for decades are in need of tidying. Set an example for how you want the rest of the company to present itself. Keep your desk clean, repaint the walls, and sell off old assets. Cleanliness sends a good message to the employees that you care about the place and want it to look nice.

In short order, you will have a much clearer sense of what is really going on in the company, everyone's personal history and work behaviors, and all the rest of the idiosyncrasies. These will largely be HR-related issues, and you will have the lay of the land. Having a clear understanding of the various players in the mix and what they each bring to the table will help you with planning and implementation down the road.

An acquisition entrepreneur recently said to me, "Once you put $2 million in someone's bank account, you start to learn what's really going on." His remark hits the nail on the head.

During the first few days, all of the little company-specific details that weren't mentioned before the closing will start to come out. The good news is that you typically learn all the relevant information very quickly. Perhaps I've been lucky, but I haven't yet found anything unexpected that wasn't manageable. This also goes back to the legal disclosure obligations in the purchase agreement, and how intently you treated the due diligence period. You should be able to greatly reduce or even eliminate any meaningful surprises.

Whenever there are employees, there are communication channels that you are not a part of, and each of those employees has questions and concerns that need to be addressed. There will be a little chaos and a constant state of motion. The only thing you can do is lead toward a vision of where the company is going and get everyone on board.

As you establish yourself as the new CEO over the first ninety days, you'll want to take a general approach of focusing the first month on the people involved, the second month on learning the processes and systems, and the third month implementing your plan of action.

DAY 1

Establishing rapport, respect, and expectations with employees, customers, and suppliers is your first initiative and will be the focus of the first month in your new role.

It begins with an all-hands meeting with your new employees and the announcement that you are the new owner. It's typical for the seller to take the floor first and deliver the news before introducing you. This meeting should be the last time the seller stands before the team they've assembled and led for years. Odds are, the majority of the staff will have heard rumors by now since due diligence in particular is such a high-touch time. They will have concerns since they don't know who the new CEO is, what changes to expect, or how those changes will impact their life.

When it's your turn to speak, keep the message simple and stick to the truth. This is your opportunity to earn the respect and trust of your new team. People loathe change, and the team will undoubtedly be concerned about changes. If nothing else, this can have an effect on productivity. It's important to address their concerns up front. Obviously, the employees will be carefully evaluating you and trying to get a sense of what type of person you are. Just as stocks are traded on future expectations, your employees are setting a virtual stock price on the company in the first meeting. They want to see that you are a human being first and can acknowledge that their livelihood is literally at stake. Don't be afraid to share your passion for the company and your excitement about the future.

The first thing your employees want to know is whether there are going to be layoffs, and the second thing they'll want to know is whether there are going to be changes in their salary or benefits. This can be a little tough because, whenever possible, new business owners hold off on any staffing or payroll decisions for at least the first ninety days. That said, you will have an intent on day one. If you have plans to change the benefits plan, this is the time to communicate that. Just "pull the bandage off." Be truthful.

If possible, I always immediately communicate that everyone will be hired, and nothing is going to change with their benefits. If you acquired a *platform* company, you bought it because of what it was already doing, and you're aware that everyone on the team played a significant part in it. Let them know you're not planning to make any major changes, especially within the first ninety to 120 days. This information will go a long way toward putting people's minds at ease and decreasing their stress.

I advise you to keep your reassurances short, sweet, and positive, and then open the floor to questions. There may not be many, but typically the group just needs a minute to warm up. The most common question I hear is some version of, "How specifically do you intend to grow the company?" Be conservative in your answer. It's better to under promise and over deliver here. You don't want to make any promises or commitments you can't keep. Let them know you are still learning and you'll rely on them to help you better understand the company they helped build. Remind them that you've only owned the company for a few hours and there is a lot of work ahead. Anchored in this reality, share your initial observations about the best pathway to growth, and convey that each of them will play a role. Everything you say here will set the tone for the first ninety days and beyond.

THE FIRST MONTH: PEOPLE

For the first thirty days, you will focus mostly on the people who make up the greater organization. Your first couple of days will likely be spent hiring all the employees into your newly formed entity and getting the human resources and payroll components in order. During the first ten days, I try to make sure I have a short, one-on-one meeting with everyone in the company. Start with management and work your way down through the organization. This gives you a chance to know everyone in the company and allows them to ask any questions they might have. You may choose to have the supervisor or manager in attendance as well; however, due to the freshness of the situation, you may prefer to have the first meeting one-on-one to eliminate any company politics that might be at play that you're not privy to.

During these short meetings, simply ask them what they do in the organization, what their background is, who they interact with, and what observations, if any, they might have for improvement in the organization as it relates to their job. Ask question like, "What would you focus on if you were in my shoes? What improvements do you think need to be made and how would you go about making them?" Often during these meetings, you can discover hidden talents or identify skillsets that can be utilized later. Above all, you'll begin to get your hands around the people that make up the organization, how they work together, and the greater culture of the company.

The only exception to a short sit down is with any sales people. Ride with your sales people instead. Understand how they work, what the marketing message is. You'll get plenty of drive time to chat.

The most important thing is that every employee feels heard and knows you are accessible to them. Not everyone agrees with me on this approach, but I share it because it has worked for me and helped to foster mutual respect and trust from the beginning. If you have developed a bold vision for the company, share it in these meetings. Let them know you want to focus on improving customer service or on-time delivery, or whatever metric they have power over that is a market differentiator. Communicate where your emphasis lies, their role in it, and begin the process of setting expectations.

It won't take long before you know who the top performers are and where the alliances are. Who shows up early and who gossips. Knowing who you can believe can help you move the company toward your vision, which is debatably the most important outcome of the first thirty days.

Customers

Although issuing a press release upon the acquisition is a great way to get top-of-mind marketing out there, you'll want to meet the top customers and suppliers before an announcement goes out. After you meet the employees, you'll want to start reaching out to the largest customers and set up meetings.

Meeting with these customers is the best way to immediately establish a customer feedback loop. How long have they been using the company? Why do they buy from this company? What are the strengths and weaknesses? Where could they improve? What is one thing they are not doing that would be of the biggest value? Who is critical to them in their interactions with the company? What would cause them to leave? Explain you'd like to have a short check-in meeting with them once a quarter to review your performance and explore opportunities to do more. If you can, determine the customer's business metrics and determine if there is a way you can impact them.

Suppliers

When meeting with suppliers, you typically want to make very clear what you need from them and how you will be evaluating their performance. Going around the sales rep and meeting the president on the first visit is a good idea. This way, if performance ever gets rocky, you'll know who to contact to get results.

Understanding any future changes from suppliers is important. Economics will have a lot to do with this. If they buy materials from overseas, for example, it could impact you if there are changes in those markets. Identify the change agents in that business so you can keep an eye on shifts in the market.

It's amazing to me how many existing suppliers will try to sell you new things immediately. It's fine to understand what they offer, but never sign any new, long-term contracts. They have a way of popping out of the woodwork and appearing urgent. If it wasn't on your list on the day before closing, it's not urgent.

THE SECOND MONTH: LEARNING

The second month should be focused on a deeper learning of all the systems and processes. How the people work together, what the metrics should be, looking for easy optimizations. From the due diligence phase, you learned at a high level how orders moved through the company, but now you can turn this to learning how the sales people work all the way through how the product is delivered and invoiced.

Learn the accounting system and order entry.

Most smaller companies rely more on people than on processes. Typically, there's one or two people in the company who have mastery over certain areas of the business. They are the go-to people in the company and have usually been there a long time. Based off of your people focus in the first month, you'll quickly identify who these people are. You should begin getting their job processes documented.

This will initiate your path of improvement by being able to have documented processes rather than depending on specific people. Consider the "bus test." If this person got hit by a bus and died, could the company function? If the answer is no, that's where you'll want to focus first.

Financially, things will be a little messy for the first few months. Among several other things, AP and AR may not line up 100 percent, checks might be deposited into the wrong account, and the inventory could be off. Get a hold of the flow of money and make sure the bank accounts are lined up properly. You want to ensure the cash is coming to you and not the previous owner. Start with accounting and watch invoices closely to ensure they are sent out in a timely manner. Put together a thirteen-week cash flow projection so you can understand your cash demands for the next quarter and get an intimate understanding of how cash cycles through the company.

The second month is a good time to consider best practices in the industry and establishing ongoing meetings with the supervisors. This is getting into the flow of operations for the first time—what your day to day will look like. Make sure you can effectively perform all of your adopted responsibilities, look for areas you need to learn, and begin looking for small, early wins.

Write an implementation plan for the future of the company and what you'll want to execute starting in month three. This can be as basic as writing a document that you reference every morning or a more sophisticated Gantt Chart with graphed timelines of each task. Either way, your implementation plan should outline:

- **Defined Goals and Objectives**: Identify what you want to accomplish and what success looks like.

- **Metrics for Success**: What is the best way to measure your results?

- **Scheduled Milestones**: Break your goal down into steps, then build a timeline that outlines when you plan to accomplish each step.

- **Allocation of Resources**: Is your plan reflected in your forecast? Do you have adequate resources to commit? This could be time, money, or personnel.

- **Team Responsibilities**: Is this all your effort, or are you planning to work with the management team of your company? Assign roles to accomplish designated groups of tasks to get more done quicker and develop teamwork toward a common goal.

Create a dashboard or a Balanced Scorecard[83] to keep track of progress and make sure you're moving the metrics that matter.

Nevertheless, allow yourself the best chance for success by creating this roadmap with the understanding that variables can impact your plan along the way. It's commonly recommended that you don't change a single thing until you have a chance to live in the business for a while and understand all the moving parts. You don't want to be reacting to problems you unknowingly caused.

THE THIRD MONTH: IMPLEMENTATION

It's not until sixty to ninety days after you've taken ownership that most would begin to make any changes: either incremental or significant. Now that you've had a couple of months to learn in depth the people and processes that make up the company, you have the

---

83   Robert S. Kaplan, D. P. Norton, *The Balanced Scorecard: Translating Strategy into Action*, Boston, MA: Harvard Business School Press, 1996.

knowledge to know how your actions can positively impact the company, as well as potential repercussions.

You can form short- and long-term goals and milestones for your organization and solidify the plan you had put together prior to acquisition. Create your vision and communicate it to your employees. This is when you begin to implement your plan. The growth driver that you bring to the table can start to go to work.

It's also the time to implement any changes you want to see. You clearly don't want to make any significant changes for a couple of months; however, if you go too long before implementing the changes you want to see, people will get comfortable and build resistance to adapting.

This is your time to shine. Launch your growth initiatives, get buy-in from your team and key customers, then dig in and start making substantial progress on your new initiative. Over time, you'll build momentum, and the future you are building will come into focus.

GROWTH THROUGH ACQUISITION

The first company I bought was my father's book printing company. He had had some success hiring sales reps from within the industry who could bring over accounts with them. I continued along this strategy but quickly saw that even well-respected, high-performing sales reps in the industry failed to bring more than a few accounts with them. By and large, the accounts stayed with our competitor and didn't transition with the rep we hired.

I also saw evidence of this as our own reps began to cycle out. Their customers stayed with us—almost 100 percent of the time. I decided to look and see what data I could find on the topic.

Although direct data was nearly impossible to locate, I was able to locate statistics that pointed to the root of what I was experiencing. Sales expert and founder of TelSmart, Josiane Feigon, reported that only 13 percent of customers felt that their sales rep understood their needs. This suggests that, assuming the product or service was solving a problem for the customer, it had nothing to do with the sales rep themselves 87 percent of the time.

Dale Carnegie observed that 91 percent of customers say they'd give referrals if asked. This supports the idea that the supplier is effective in providing value, but where does that value come from? The sales rep plays a role in execution, but the value proposition of the product or service itself is the root provider of value. In other words, should the sales rep leave, close to 100 percent of the value is still being realized by the company, almost all of the time.

Still, when reps leave to go work at a competing entity, their intent is clearly to attempt to attract customers they've worked with in the past. Our current customers. So, keeping a sales rep from leaving in the first place rewards the company by decreasing the intent of pulling existing customers away.

ACQUIRE NEW SALES REPS WITH CUSTOMERS SIMULTANEOUSLY

Instead of trying to locate and attract established industry reps to your company, what would it look like to acquire the competition outright, taking over the service of their customers, brand, and sales reps?

Consider this. Say you're trying to find new sales reps who can generate new revenue of $1 million per new rep. If you could find enough of them, you'd likely hire as many as you could afford, right? You might be willing to hire three to five reps over the next twelve months, for example. Three to five new reps would then equate to $3 to $5 million in revenue, right? Who doesn't want to grow by $4 million?

If you could locate a competitor selling around $4 million, who was ready to sell, you could accomplish this goal in one day.

Running the math will show you that acquiring a firm generating $4 million in revenue could be acquired for a minimum down payment around $180,000. Oddly, you may need to pay close to $180,000 for a single rep if they're able to sell $1 million in new business every year. The calculation is promising.

It also eliminates the risk of a costly mis-hire or a new rep leaving the company just after you paid for all their "training." Growing through acquisition can make more sense than trying to grow organically through sales efforts.

AFFORDABLY ACQUIRE NEW INFRASTRUCTURE AND CAPITALIZE ON INDUSTRY TRENDS

Often, acquisition can accomplish more than just growth goals. While in the printing industry, I saw that traditional "offset" production was declining, and "digital" print services had been growing steadily at almost 30 percent year over year for the past five years. It was clear this trend had taken hold and was going to continue.

I had installed a digital printing department inside the company and we quickly grew it to one of the largest in the state. But growth had stalled. We lacked the IT infrastructure to scale it beyond our high-touch sales and production processes. When pricing out what the new infrastructure would cost to build, it was intimidating.

It was not only a big number, but it didn't come with any customers. Meaning it could use up our cash, but not provide any additional sales without changing our marketing expertise as well. It frankly would put the company at too much risk. It looked a lot like, well, a startup.

I realized that, if I was able to find a company with the digital infrastructure I wanted already in place, then I might be able to acquire a profitable infrastructure that could bridge our company into a new product line and capture a trend taking hold in the industry. Since digital was still young, many of the new digital-only companies were short on internal expertise and, due to growth and capital equipment costs, cash flow was challenging. As a result, they may be open to selling.

I decided if I could purchase one that had exceeded $1 million in revenue, then, as we learned in Chapter 1, the product-market fit had hit a minimum viable proven level. A profile like this would be an interesting acquisition. In theory, we would be acquiring a profitable, revenue-generating infrastructure, rather than building the costly infrastructure from scratch.

In addition, an acquisition would cost a fraction of what building the infrastructure from scratch would cost. This is because when you acquire a company, you pay a multiple of the cash flow the business is generating, then use debt vehicles to cover a percentage of the cost. When you build infrastructure, you need invested capital to cover the buildout.

Growing through acquisition can be faster and more affordable than expanding organic sales efforts or building out new, unproven product lines.

Seeing that my current company was already profitable, I wouldn't require any additional income from the acquired company. The cash flow could be used 100 percent to pay down the debt and reinvest in the growth of the company. This would accelerate the strength and reach of the company, and maintain a margin of safety—something new hires, new product development, and new startups lack.

ACQUISITION AS AN EXIT STRATEGY

I recruited a lower middle-market advisor to work with me in contacting the right organizations. I showed up with a list of companies providing either traditional or disruptive services in my space. After twenty-four months of searching, we found the absolute perfect fit. They had everything I was looking for: millions in revenue, one of the best custom-built IT infrastructures in the industry, and a production line that did everything ours didn't. We needed each other.

The only problem was that this acquisition target was not for sale. We approached them proactively, so discussions took months. It ended with the CEO of the other company saying, "Well, we absolutely have to do this. I just want to change one thing—I want to buy you."

It was the following months where I realized trying to *grow* through acquisition was also a very good way to *exit* a company, which is the ultimate goal of most companies—including every startup that's ever accepted outside investment.

HOW TO GROW

Ultimately, there are three ways to grow a company. You need to get more customers, you need to increase the order frequency of the customers you have, or you need to increase the average order value per customer.

This can be done through adding products or services, expanding geographically, bundling products together, and increasing the quality of sales and marketing efforts, but at the end of the day it requires an offering that delivers value to customers. Over the last ten years, I've been lucky enough to acquire for infrastructure, customer relationship, geographic expansion, local growth, and new product development. There are truly no limits to the benefits of this approach, and the opportunities seem endless for the ambitious.

This is an added benefit you'll receive from taking your efforts to position yourself upstream. You'll still be privy to the activity. Just now, as I was finishing writing his chapter, I decided to open my email. This morning alone, I received thirteen newly listed companies from three firms. These range from $98,000 in SDE to $98 million in revenue. From software to consulting to manufacturing and retail. Literally any kind of business you want to be in is out there and established—you just need to find the right one for you.

When you adopt the acquisition entrepreneurship philosophy and buy then build rather than start from scratch, you're able to begin with a profitable infrastructure and grow from there. It's the entrepreneurship hack that I learned on my journey. There is no reason why you can't do it too.

ACQUISITION IN THE ENTREPRENEURSHIP ECONOMY

"What about ten times more entrepreneurship?"

-TAYLOR PEARSON,
FROM *THE END OF JOBS*

In this book, we've covered how buying an existing business can be a better model of entrepreneurship simply because it provides a profitable infrastructure, complete with customers, historical performance, and a margin of safety from which to "launch" your own initiatives and leadership.

We've observed how business ownership is the best method for engineering real wealth for most people. And how finding the right opportunity for *you* allows for maximizing the impact of your strengths and skillsets to build value. All while enjoying engaged and fulfilling work.

We've discussed the best way to define what you are looking for, not by industry or revenue size but by opportunity and discretionary earnings. And we've seen how to find the best opportunities.

By getting yourself "upstream" and making yourself a hub of deal flow, you can get first look at new listings as they become available.

We've discussed how to navigate a deal, what to expect from the seller, and outlined a structure for your transition to CEO. Perhaps more importantly, we've given you a blueprint to design your future as an acquisition entrepreneur.

Acquisition entrepreneurship is not going to be the right approach for every business idea. But most of the time, it's a better way to engineer the necessary success in the first place. By acquiring an infrastructure that produces profitable revenue, you save months (more typically years) of time raising capital. You put the emphasis on leading a successful organization as soon as possible so you can get started *building*, rather than focusing on surviving the startup phase.

Finally, by taking the risk yourself, by putting your own invested dollars and borrowed capital into a company, you own the whole company. This aligns the financial rewards and upside potential with your own efforts, rather than letting outside investors gain the financial benefits of your labor.

THE ENTREPRENEUR'S ECONOMY

Ron Davison's book, *The Fourth Economy*, reviews the economic development of the western world through the lens of Eli Goldratt's notorious *Theory of Constraints*. Davison observes that as economic periods transitioned from Agricultural to Industrial to Knowledge, additional investments in the previous economic drivers resulted in diminishing returns.

The transition from one period to the next was instead driven by capitalizing on the next limitation. Land was the limiter that gave birth to the Agricultural period; access to capital was the limiter that drove the Industrial period; and education was the limiter that produced the Knowledge period. But since 2000, with land easily accessible, capital in abundance, and the saturation of advanced education unable to produce higher pay rates, a new limiter has emerged.

"Right now," says Davison, "becoming an entrepreneur is like becoming a knowledge worker in 1900. That is, it is possible but hard enough that few people do it."

Entrepreneurship is the next limiter to be conquered. As the economy shifts, entrepreneurial skills will, like never before, define the forefront of economic development. Said another way, entrepreneurship is the key to success in the current economy.

Simultaneously, there is an enormous transition, never before seen in history, occurring right now. Baby boomers, who own more companies than any other generation in history, are retiring in droves—$10 trillion in business value will need to change hands, with the highest volume of opportunity in businesses below $5 million in revenue. As we covered in the first chapter, only 4 percent of companies in the United States achieve $1 million in revenue. Literally, it's some of the top performing companies in the world that are coming up for sale. This happens to be occurring at the same exact time that entrepreneurship has become the new driver for the next economic period.

The convergence of these to historical moments of entrepreneurship defining the economic frontier, and the retiring baby boomer tsunami presents a unique opportunity for those ambitious enough to tackle acquisition entrepreneurship.

In fact, as Taylor Pearson underscores in his entrepreneurship manifesto, *The End of Jobs*, jobs as we've come to know them are becoming less and less available. Since 2000, the population has grown 240 percent faster than job growth.

The question, Pearson provides, is no longer "How do I get a job doing that?" It's, "How do I *create* a job doing that?" Creating opportunity and building value are skillsets. And they are driving the new economy.

Entrepreneurship isn't just popular anymore, it's necessary. Acquisition entrepreneurship provides a career accelerator for people going out on their own. It provides infrastructure beyond just one person.

As we've seen, startups fail. Almost all of them. Out of the ones that do make it, the vast majority get stuck in low revenue companies, never scaling to much beyond the efforts of their owners. By buying these companies, you create your own platform without the associated risk of a startup. You can grow organically, innovate through adding new products, or scale with additional acquisitions. The model reduces risk and provides multiple outlets for building value. Acquiring a business is the fastest route to success in the entrepreneurship game.

It doesn't take long to be the CEO of your own successful company. You can be there in six to nine months, it just takes commitment to the goal and the courage to take the first step.

We've covered the *why*, the *what*, and the *how* of acquisition entrepreneurship. You know enough at this point to know if this avenue is right for you, and by going through the exercises in this book, you know more and are more prepared than the vast majority of potential buyers.

If it's right, I encourage you to get started on this path as soon as possible. It will change your life forever, and you will never look back. Owning a business is rewarding in a way that books can only point to. While describing their lifestyle, most entrepreneurs relish in the autonomy and financial benefits of owning a company. But it goes beyond that. When you own a company, your company becomes an extension of you. It engulfs your spirit, mind, and body. When you breathe, you breathe your company. When your company thrives, you thrive. A spiritual integration occurs that leads to the most engaged life I have ever witnessed. Perhaps we see proof of this in the many masterminds, forums, and communities that have been built around this one shared experience.

Why acquisition hasn't penetrated the entrepreneurship community much beyond the elite universities is surprising. But often, that's where the best ideas originate. Acquisition entrepreneurship is truly the startup hack, or the shorted path to the desired destination. I wrote this book not because I wanted to but because I had to. Adding acquisition to the practice of entrepreneurship offers so many advantages that I needed to share it. If this book has made you aware of, helped you see with more clarity, or inspired you to take the first step toward a life of acquisition entrepreneurship, it's done its job. A life of passion awaits you.

BIBLIOGRAPHY

Bartlett, Joseph W. *Fundamentals of Venture Capital*. Lanham: Madison Books, 1999.

Besanko, David, et al. *Economics of Strategy*. New York: Wiley Custom, 2000.

Blank, . Steven G. *The Four Steps to the Epiphany: Successful Strategies for Products That Win*. S.G. Blank, 2007.

Christensen, Clayton M. *The Innovator's Dilemma: When New Technologies Cause Great Firms to Fail*. 1st HarperBusiness ed. New York: HarperBusiness, 2000.

Collins, James C. *Good to Great: Why Some Companies Make the Leap ... and Others Don't*. New York, NY: HarperBusiness, 2001.

Collins, James C. *How the mighty fall: and why some companies never give in*. New York: Harper Collins, 2009

Crabtree, Greg and, Beverly B Harzog. *Simple numbers, straight talk, big profits!: 4 keys to unlock your business potential*. Austin: Greenleaf Book Group Press, 2011

Dawn Langkamp Bolton Michelle D. Lane, (2012),"Individual entrepreneurial orientation: development of a measurement instrument", Education + Training, Vol. 54 Iss 2/3 pp. 219 - 233

Gibson, John V. M. *How to Buy a Business without Being Had: Successfully Negotiating the Purchase of a Small Business* Bloomington: Trafford, 2010

Graham, Benjamin, *The Intelligent Investor: a Book of Practical Counsel.* New York :Harper, 1973.

Harnish, Verne *Scaling up: how a few companies make it ... and why the rest don't.* Ashburn: Gazelles Inc., 2015 http://dx.doi.org/10.1108/00400911211210314

Ismail, Salim *Exponential organizations: why new organizations are ten times better, faster, and cheaper than yours (and what to do about it).* New York : First Diversion, 2014

Jackim,Richard E. and Peter G. Christman *The $10 trillion opportunity: designing successful exit strategies for middle market business owners: a guide for professional advisors* Palatine: Exit Planning Institute, 2005

Joseph, Richard A., Anna M. Nekoranec and Carl H. Steffens *How to buy a business: entrepreneurship through acquisition* Chicago: Dearborn Financial Pub., 1993

Kawasaki,Guy *The art of the start: the time-tested, battle-hardened guide for anyone starting anything*. New York: Penguin Group, 2004

Keller, Gary, et al. *The Millionaire Real Estate Investor: Anyone Can Do It--Not Everyone Will*. New York: McGraw-Hill, 2005.

Marks, Kenneth H., Robert T. Slee, Christian W. Blees and Michael R. Nall *Middle market M & A: handbook for investment banking and business consulting* Hoboken: Wiley and Sons Inc., 2012

Osterwalder, Alexander and Yves Pigneur Business model generation a handbook for visionaries, game changers, and challengers Hoboken: Wiley & Sons, 2010

Parker, Richard *How to Buy a Good Business at a Great Price* Fort Lauderdale:Diomo, 2013

Peters, Basil *Early exits: exit strategies for entrepreneurs and angel investors (but maybe not venture capitalists)*. Canada: MeteorBytes, 2009.

Porter, M. E. Competitive Strategy: Techniques for Analyzing Industries and Competitors. New York: Free Press, 1980

Rath, Tom. *StrengthsFinder 2.0* New York: Gallop Inc., 2007

Ries, Eric. *The Lean Startup: How Today's Entrepreneurs Use Continuous Innovation to Create Radically Successful Businesses*. New York: Crown Business, 2011.

Ruback, Richard and Yudkoff Royce. *HBR Guide to Buying a Small Business*. Harvard Business Review Press, 2017.

Seligman, Martin E. P. *Flourish: A Visionary New Understanding of Happiness and Well-Being*. 2013. Print.

Shapiro, Alan C., and Sheldon D. Balbirer. *Modern Corporate Finance: a Multidisciplinary Approach to Value Creation*. New Jersey: Prentice Hall, 2000.

Short, Kevin M. and Kathryn A. Bolinske *Sell your business for an outrageous price: an insider's guide to getting more than you ever thought possible* New York: American Management Association, 2015

Siwan Mitchelmore, Jennifer Rowley, (2010) "Entrepreneurial competencies: a literature review and development agenda", International Journal of Entrepreneurial Behavior & Research, Vol. 16 Issue: 2, pp.92-111, https://doi.org/10.1108/13552551011026995

Stanley, Thomas J., and William D. Danko. *The Millionaire Next Door: The Surprising Secrets of America's Wealthy*. 1st Taylor Trade Pub. ed. Lanham, Md.: Taylor Trade Pub., 2010.

Stieglitz, Richard G. and Stuart H. Sorkin *Expensive mistakes when buying & selling companies: ... and how to avoid them in your deals* Potomac: Acuity Publishing, 2010

Thakor, Anjan V. *Becoming a Better Value Creator: How to Improve the Company's Bottom Line--and Your Own.* San Francisco: Jossey Bass Inc, 2000.

Timmons, Jeffry A. *New Venture Creation: Entrepreneurship for the 21st Century.* Irwin/McGraw-Hill, 1999.

Vesa Taatila, Samuel Down, (2012) "Measuring entrepreneurial orientation of university students", Education + Training, Vol. 54 Issue: 8/9, pp.744-760, https://doi.org/10.1108/00400911211274864

Warrillow, *John Built to sell: creating a business that can thrive without you.* New York: Portfolio/Penguin, 2011

Zhao, H., & Seibert, S. E. (2006). The Big Five personality dimensions and entrepreneurial status: A meta-analytical review. Journal of Applied Psychology, 91(2), 259-271. http://dx.doi.org/10.1037/0021-9010.91.2.259

ACKNOWLEDGEMENTS

MY NAME IS ON THE COVER OF THIS BOOK BUT I ALL I DID WAS surround myself with great people and connect dots that already existed. So many greater than I have helped me understand entrepreneurship, investing, the private markets, acquisition, exiting, business strategy, psychology, how to grow companies, and the creation of this book.

First, please understand that nothing would happen without my jaw-droppingly amazing wife. Colleen is beautiful, hardworking, and fiercely intelligent. Living with her, and our three very resourceful girls, fills me with immense gratitude and joy daily. Without her enduring support and never-ending ability to shore up my many shortcomings, neither my choice of work nor this book would be possible. Thank you for all that you are, Colleen (…and for giving birth to those three little startups).

My grandfathers, Bob Deibel and Frank Corley, were the original acquisition entrepreneurs. They set the stage for progress through this adventure before I was old enough to know that I had opposable thumbs. We walk the path now that has been cleared by the generations before us. Acquisition entrepreneurship, although seen today in new light, was embodied by great business owners like these decades ago.

I need to thank my many business partners. Anywhere in this book where the word "I" is used, I assure you it is a "we." Business is a team sport and I have been so fortunate to surround myself with superhuman and amazing partners. Don't think this is limited to business partners, but also managers, co-investors, and employees. Everyday our businesses grow and thrive because of your thoughtful input and dedicated effort. Together we build.

Chad Troutwine for his truly limitless inspiration and encouragement. He was the first one I spoke to about the concept of *Buy Then Build* and he has been watering the seed with his gregarious enthusiasm and insightful and intelligent advice for years. Chad is a force of nature, a great business partner, and a true friend.

I have immense gratitude for Ken Harrington, the founding Managing Director of the Skandalaris Center for Innovation and Entrepreneurship at Washington University in St. Louis. One couldn't ask for a better mentor and teacher for entrepreneurship. Ken's approach values both academic and real-life experiences, which culminate into a whole greater than its parts. Ken taught me much of my foundational understanding of entrepreneurship, venture capital, and private equity, and he has built one of the best entrepreneurship programs in the world.

The managing director of the Kingsley Group, Gary Rogers, has been a godsend. At times, Gary has been my closest partner, both in executing business strategy and the buying and selling of businesses. If there is anything in this book about businesses transactions that is worth reading, it likely originated with Gary.

I am so thankful for Michal Nall, for creating the Alliance of M&A Advisors and the Certified M&A Advisor program. I received both a quantitative understanding of the private capital markets, training in best practices in M&A Advisory, and access to an expansive network of middle market M&A Advisors. He coauthored the textbooks *Middle Market M&A: Handbook for Investment Banking and Business Consulting* with Kenneth Marks, Robert Slee, and Christian Blees, which is the quintessential book on the subject for middle market advisors. He is a wealth of knowledge and eager to share it with the world.

I've met Tom West on a phone call about 10 years ago. I'm pretty sure this is the first and last time we spoke, but Tom is responsible for the International Business Broker Association, the Certified Business Intermediary program, and is the grandfather of the M&A Master Intermediary program. He's also the founder of the Business brokerage Press and some of the best tools in the industry for lower middle market and main street transactions. Tom has done so much to create a culture of best practices to the otherwise fragmented broker community that he needs to be recognized.

I received tremendous insights and help from both David Weller, Principal at Leadership Alliance, and Allie Taylor, partner at Orange Kiwi, around the psychological make-up of successful entrepreneurs and CEOs. David is a close friend and a brilliant mind whose assessments have helped me find some of the best talent I've ever worked with. He's also responsible for introducing me to the work of Martin Seligman, which probably cost me a year of my life as I dove headfirst into reading everything I could about positive psychology.

I want to thank Mark Daoust, founder and CEO at Quiet Light Brokerage for not only building the best firm for buying and selling online businesses in the world, but also for his endless hours helping me navigate and learn the specifics of this niche. Quiet Light leads the industry in online business transactions and it's due to Mark's "true North" compass. He embodies everything that you could ask for in an Advisor.

In the same regard Joe Valley, also at Quiet Light, is a true master. Joe and I started working together just after the last edit of this book was written. Joe makes transactions look like art, and he has so much to share.

Champ Davis and John Olsen at Davis Capital got into the weeds with me on a deal that never closed. If there is ever an Olympic team of the best middle market advisors assembled, the gang at Davis Capital will be on it. They have a sixth sense for business opportunity and know how to get it done with wall street professionalism and the passion of true entrepreneurs.

Martin Myers and Mike Nichols at PE Partners for living the truth that the best partnerships go beyond capital. These guys live at the intersection of entrepreneurship and deal-making and are building a market network with remarkable qualities. I've enjoyed our work immensely and the many remarkable relationships it's lead to.

Jeff Stockton at the Olin Business School at Washington University in St. Louis, whose help in the research for this book helped firm up many of the hypotheses. Eric Jones and Max Byers, MBAs from the Olin school for their early enthusiasm and help on the project.

Thank you so much to the Entrepreneur's Organization in St. Louis. The community has been so rich, insightful, and supportive. Especially, Cheryl Lauer for granting me a spot on the board, Jim Guller for suckering me into taking on all the Accelerator program events, and the entire Bootstapper forum lineage (but especially David, Carl, Dan, Howard, the other David, Jim, Tom, Don, Gretchen, Jackie, and Nick). You've been the essential compass to navigating these entrepreneurial waters at the darkest times and applying the right pressure to level up. Please continue to show us all how it's done.

The team at Scribe Media and Lioncrest Publishing for helping me get this book finished and published. It was a behemoth undertaking and their balance of assistance and inspiration was perfectly executed. Hal Clifford for confirming and fine tuning my outline, Brooke White for getting me to a final first draft (finally), Erin Tyler for the perfect cover, and Tucker Max for the tough love at all the right times. If there is a single word in this book that shouldn't be there, trust me that Tucker told me with conviction to remove it.

My Publishing Manager Katherine Sears could not have been a better partner. She started Booktrope, a disruptive market network for self-published authors. After raising over seven figures of capital and going through Y-Combinator, the # 1 accelerator program in the world, she met early success. After almost two years of running a successful, aggressively growing company she was faced with a change in product-market fit, and the startup capitulated through no fault of her team. She understands first-hand how a great product, all-star team, world class training, and amazing idea can fail in execution from external sources. Oh yeah, and she's a publishing rock star. Thank you so much.

Ben LeClair is my true partner in crime and biggest cheerleader. He constantly reminds me of the next level of explosive success right around the corner. Ben is not only my lifeline but a great producer who's input steered the rudder of early drafts of this book.

Doveed Linder really doesn't give a shit what you think. He's going to write and make films and author one of the best books on boxing. The guy literally gets in the boxing ring. A never-ending inspiration of what it's like to live a life of bull-headed effort. For me entrepreneurship and filmmaking are inseparable. Doveed has always embodied bootstrapping at its finest and he showed me first-hand how do to it in the 90's.

Garrett Gunderson, Shep Hyken, Cliff Holekamp, and Taylor Pearson for offering advanced praise for my first book. That takes tremendous courage! Fast friends in every instance and guidance along the way. Thank you.

My parents have supported me at every step for over 40 years. I am so blessed. This of course includes tender stories from my childhood and numerous tales from my defiant adolescence (I'm an entrepreneur and, hey, rules don't really apply to me). Ultimately, our relationship evolved into a partnership filled with immense love and respect. My parents sold me the first company I bought. Being on the "same side of the table" as the seller helped me learn the transaction process without having to worry about the potential "getting-ripped-off" component. I'm sure, if I had tried to buy from anyone else in the world I never would have bought a company. This experience gave me great insight as to the barriers-to-entry that exist for would be acquisition entrepreneurs. Perhaps this is all their fault.

Finally, to all the entrepreneurs I have met along the way. You make life so rich.

ABOUT THE AUTHOR

WALKER DEIBEL is an entrepreneur and investor who has co-founded three startups, acquired seven companies, and consulted or participated in over 100 business transactions. After the success of *Buy Then Build*, he started an elite accelerator for acquisition entrepreneurs, the Acquisition Lab. He holds an MBA from the Olin School of Business at Washington University in St. Louis, where he received the Declaration of Accomplishment in Entrepreneurship award from the Skandalaris Center of Innovation and Entrepreneurship. Walker is a Certified M&A Advisor and former SEC-licensed stockbroker. He was awarded Thought Leader of the Year by the Alliance of M&A Advisors for his work on *Buy Then Build* and its adoption into universities. He lives in St. Louis, Missouri, with his wife and their three resourceful children. Learn more about acquisition entrepreneurship at BuyThenBuild.com.

CPSIA information can be obtained
at www.ICGtesting.com
Printed in the USA
LVHW042058290623
751028LV00030B/974/J